HD

TRIBUTE TO FREUD

WRITING ON THE WALL · ADVENT

FOREWORD BY
NORMAN HOLMES PEARSON

D0062904

A NEW DIRECTIONS BOOK

Library of Congress Cataloging in Publication Data
H. D. (Hilda Doolittle), 1886-1961.
 Tribute to Freud.
 (A New Directions Book)
 Originally published: Boston : D.R. Godine, c1974.
 Includes bibliographical references.
 1. H. D. (Hilda Doolittle), 1886-1961. 2. Psychotherapy patients—
United States—Biography. 3. Psychoanalysis—Case studies. 4. Freud, Sigmund,
1856-1939. I. Title.
RC464.H2A37 1984   616.89'17   84-3317
ISBN 0-8112-0897-4 (pbk.)

Manufactured in the United States of America
This edition is published by arrangement with David R. Godine, Publisher
First published as New Directions Paperbook 572 in 1984
Published simultaneously in Canada by George J. McLeod, Ltd, Toronto

New Directions Books are published for James Laughlin
by New Directions Publishing Corporation
80 Eighth Avenue, New York 10011

TABLE OF CONTENTS

FOREWORD

'THE PAST IS literally blasted into consciousness with the Blitz
in London,' H.D. said. Her sessions with Sigmund Freud,
when she first wrote about them in 1944, were a part of the
past. With him, the desk and walls of his consulting room
filled with bibelots which were tokens of history, she had gone
back to her childhood, back to the breakup of her marriage
and the birth of her child, back to the death of her brother in
service in France, and the consequent death, from shock, of
her father, and back to the breakup of her literary circle in
London – Aldington, Pound, Lawrence, each gone his way. In
the Vienna of the early 1930s, with its lengthening shadows,
she was putting together the shards of her own history, facing
a new war, knowing it would come, fearing it as she had feared
its predecessor.

Freud helped her to remember and to understand what she
remembered. When she composed 'Writing on the Wall,'
published in book form as *Tribute to Freud*, the war had come.
Destruction was not a threat but a reality. Experience was a
palimpsest. Again she recognized for herself the importance
of persistence in remembering. Remembering Freud was significant, for remembering him was remembering what she
had remembered with him. 'For me, it was so important,' she
wrote, repeating, 'it was so important, my own LEGEND. Yes,
my own LEGEND. Then, to get well and re-create it.' She used
'legend' multiply – as story, a history, an account, a thing for
reading, her own myth. H.D.'s war years brought an astonishing revitalization. Silent in a sense for years, suddenly

she wrote her war trilogy, several novels and short stories which are still unpublished, the text of *By Avon River*, drafts of *Bid Me to Live*, and *Tribute to Freud*. They were re-creations. All literature is.

The earlier version of *Tribute to Freud* has been out of print in America. Its reputation and its fascination as an informal portrait of the great psychoanalyst have persisted. In the past two years an English edition has appeared, as well as a French and an Italian translation. A German translation will appear shortly. Ernest Jones, Freud's biographer, reviewed the 1956 publication in *The International Journal of Psycho-Analysis*. He set a tone. 'The book, with its appropriate title,' he said, 'is surely the most delightful and precious appreciation of Freud's personality that is ever likely to be written. Only a fine creative artist could have written it. It is like a lovely flower, and the crude pen of a scientist hesitates to profane it by attempting to describe it. I can only say that I envy anyone who has not yet read it, and that it will live as the most enchanting ornament of all the Freudian biographical literature.' H.D. was pleased. She would have been pleased by its most recent praise; Norman Holland in his *Poems in Persons* (1973), a psychoanalytic study of the creation and reception of poetry, says, 'I know of no account by an analysand that tells more about Freud, his techniques, or the analytic experience as it seems from within.' This expanded version of *Tribute to Freud* tells still more.

'Writing on the Wall' was written, as she says in her prefatory note, 'with no reference to the Vienna note-books of spring 1933.' These had remained in Switzerland. It was when she returned to Lausanne after the war and recovered the notebooks that she wrote ' "Advent," the continuation of "Writing on the Wall," or its prelude.' The original had been a meditation; 'Advent' was its gloss. This more personally detailed section was omitted from the originally published book. Now, however, it is appropriate to include the second part, in which she comments on 'Writing on the Wall' as well as expands herself and the significance of self. 'Advent' is testimony.

'I am on the fringes or in the penumbra of the light of my father's science and my mother's art – the psychology or philosophy of Sigmund Freud,' she wrote in 'Advent.' 'I must find new words as the Professor found or coined new words to explain certain as yet unrecorded states of mind or being!' There had been recordings, of course, Freud's own or like Otto Rank's *The Myth of the Birth of the Hero,* which Freud shrewdly recommended to her when she told him of her dream of the Egyptian princess and the child afloat in the bulrushes. But Freud does, she wrote, 'follow the workings of my creative mind.' Freud knew she had to make her own recordings. No one else could do that for her. Freud had a passionate concern with the ontogeny of art. It was by no accident that the theosophist van der Leeuw and H.D. had contemporary hours on the Berggasse.

'I begin intensive reading of psychoanalytic journals, books and study Sigmund Freud,' she wrote in 1932. 'There is talk of my possibly going to Freud himself in Vienna.' The one who principally talked was Freud's distinguished student and member of the Circle, Dr. Hanns Sachs, whom H.D. had known in Berlin and with whom she had had sessions. Earlier than these, and less satisfactory, were some twenty-four sessions in 1931 in London with Mary Chadwick, to whom she had gone when the collapse of a friend threatened her own collapse. Still earlier had been the informal conversations with Havelock Ellis in Brixton at the close of World War One. He had traveled, later, in 1920, on the same boat with Bryher and herself to Malta and Greece. The companionship seems to have made no memorable impact on any of them. Disappointed in his indifference to her manuscript 'Notes on Thought and Vision,' she remembered him chiefly in terms of Norman Douglas' *mot*: 'He is a man with one eye in the country of the blind.'

In Freud's fuller vision she found both stimulation and encouragement. Years later than either 'Writing on the Wall' or 'Advent' she returned again to his memory. The end of her life was near, and she was hospitalized with a broken hip. 'Of course,' she wrote, 'as the Professor said, "there is always something more to find out." I felt that he was speaking for himself (an informal moment as I was about to leave). It was almost as if something I had said was *new*, that he even felt that I was a *new* experience. He must have thought the same of everyone, but I felt his personal delight, I was *new*. Everyone else was *new*, every dream and dream association was *new*. After the years and years of patient, plodding research, it was all *new*.'

Newness was what happened to Freud's bibelots and H.D.'s remembering when their contexts changed. We are always remaking history. Returning to the details of her childhood, in Freud's consulting room, surrounded by his little treasures, she was redefining both her childhood and them. '"My mother, my mother," I cry,' she noted of a dream, 'I sob violently, tears, tears, tears.' Her mother was Moravian, and allied to the Mystery and to love feasts; her mother painted, she was musical, and it was she who gave his first musical training to her brother, H.D.'s uncle, J. Fred Wolle, who later studied organ and counterpoint in Munich and was, in H.D.'s Bethlehem childhood, organist of the Moravian church. He established the now seventy-five-year-old Bach Festivals for which Bethlehem is chiefly known today. H.D.'s grandfather (Papalie), the Rev. Francis Wolle, was the author of *Desmids of the United States* (1884), the well-known

Freshwater Algae of the United States (1887), and *Diatomaceae of North America* (1890). He used the microscope, but more significantly to his family he had been for twenty years, until his retirement in 1881, head of the Moravian Seminary. H.D.'s ambience was Moravian.

Her father was older and, as she repeatedly inferred, from 'outside.' H.D. was the child of the second marriage of a widower. He was a middle-western New Englander; he taught mathematics; he was an astronomer who mapped the stars at night and napped until noon. 'I never had a letter from him in my life, but our mother shared her letters from him, on rare occasions when he was away from home. He would write whimsical, rhymed verses sometimes.'

She was her father's favorite, her older brother was her mother's, she felt. 'But the mother is the Muse, the Creator, and in my case especially, as my mother's name was Helen.' 'Obviously,' she wrote in 'Advent,' 'this is my inheritance. I derive my imaginative faculties through my musician-artist mother.' But the inheritance was not simple. ' "My mother, my mother," I cry. . . .' As she wrote elsewhere, 'She only felt that she [was] a disappointment to her father, an odd duckling to her mother.'

Charles Doolittle was born in 1843. His first marriage took place in Michigan in 1866; his second, to Helen Wolle, in 1882. He was 43 when H.D. was born, and Professor of Mathematics and Astronomy at Lehigh. From 1895 to 1912 he was Professor of Astronomy at the University of Pennsylvania and Director of the Flower Astronomical Observatory in Upper Darby, on the outskirts of Philadelphia. He was a scientist with honorary degrees, and the author both of monographs on the results of observations with the Zenith telescope, and of *Practical Astronomy as Applied to Geodesy and Navigation* (1885). His son Eric (1869–1920) succeeded him both to the professorship and to the directorship of the observatory.

H.D. as a girl sometimes thought of William Morris as a spiritual father. 'This is the god-father that I never had. . . . I did not know much about him until I was (as I say) about sixteen. I was given a book of his to read, by Miss Pitcher, at Miss Gordon's school; – a little later, Ezra Pound read the poetry to me. The book Miss Pitcher gave me was on furniture, perhaps an odd introduction. But my father had made a bench for my room, some bookcases downstairs, from William Morris designs. My father had been a carpenter's apprentice, as a boy. This "William Morris" father might have sent me to an art school but the Professor of Astronomy and Mathematics insisted on my preparing for college. He wanted eventually (he even said so) to make a mathematician of me, a research worker or scientist like (he even said so) Madame Curie. He did make a research worker of me but in another dimension. It was a long time before I found William Morris and that was by accident, though we are told that "nothing occurs accidentally." I must choose, because my life depends upon it, between the artist and the scientist. I manage in the second year of college to have a slight breakdown and I manage to get engaged to Ezra Pound.'

She made her choice. Her parents objected to Pound as a son-in-law. She had left Bryn Mawr, then she left Philadelphia for New York, and then left New York for London. Henceforth she was alone. She wanted her mother but she wanted her father too. Both figured in her 'legend.' Her poem 'Tribute to the Angels' was written in the same year as 'Writing on the Wall.' In it she asks,

> *what is this mother-father*
> *to tear at our entrails?*
> *what is this unsatisfied duality*
> *which you can not satisfy?*

'The house in some indescribable way,' she wrote in 'Advent,' 'depends on father-mother. At the point of integration or regeneration, there is no conflict over rival loyalties.' This was the integration she sought, the point at which she could say, having memory with understanding, 'I owned myself.'

The breaking-away, however, had been a necessary step. Looking back, in 1950, she wrote me, 'I don't suppose it was the fault of Bryn Mawr that I didn't like it. My second year was broken into or across by my affair with E.P., who after all, at that time, proved a stimulus and was the scorpionic sting or urge that got me away – at that time it was essential. I felt there I had fallen between two stools, what with my mother's musical connection and my father's and half-brother's stars! I did find my path – thanks partly to E.P., also R.A., Lawrence and the rest.'

But she separated from Richard Aldington and, finally, divorced him. The story she has told in *Bid Me to Live*. Aldington had already given his version in *Death of a Hero*. It was the subject of John Cournos' *Miranda Masters*. D. H. Lawrence touched on it briefly in *Aaron's Rod*. Few episodes have been so amply treated.

Lawrence appears frequently in *Tribute to Freud*, especially with reference to his story, 'The Man Who Died.' In *Bid Me to Live* he plays a significant role. He had the *gloire*. But her reference in 'Advent' to their leave-taking is enigmatic: ' "I hope never to see you again," he wrote in that last letter.' Perhaps her comments to herself after reading Harry Moore's biography of Lawrence have some relevance. 'I have read,' she said, 'the last two-thirds of the book, painstakingly reviewing my own feelings. I find confirmation of certain problems of my own, for instance, about Freud. Lawrence was instinctively against Sigmund Freud, Frieda was intelligently for him. But it was long before I had "come" to Freud that Frieda spoke to me of "love." It was in the *Madrigal* [*Bid Me to Live*] drawing-room, but did not come into my romance. Frieda and I were alone together in the big room. Frieda said that she had had a friend, an older man, who had told her that "if love is free, everything is free." There had been the scene the night before or shortly before, in which Lawrence said that Frieda was there for ever on his right hand, I was *there* for ever – on his left. Frieda said when we were alone, "but Lawrence does not really care for women. He only cares for men. Hilda, *you have no idea of what he is like.*" '

Pound's belligerent disapproval of Freud cooled their friendship, though it was rewarmed during the St. Elizabeth years. An unpublished letter from Pound to H.D. in 1954 gives the tone of his disapproval. 'I can't blow everybodies' noses for 'em,' he wrote. 'Have felt yr / vile Freud all bunk / but the silly Xristers bury all their good authors / ... instead of sticking to reading list left by Dante / ...You got into the wrong pig stye, ma chère. But not too late to climb out.'*

Others never quite took the places of these three. Stephen Haden-Guest was a more casual friend. Arthur Waley was at best an acquaintance. Kenneth Macpherson, Bryher's husband, was much closer. H.D. liked his novels as well as his company. With him as film director she acted with Paul Robeson in *Borderline*. To *Close-Up*, of which Macpherson was an editor, she contributed articles on the cinema. But none of these, nor others later, had the *gloire*. Freud was the exception.

J. J. van der Leeuw was a symbol rather than a person. H.D. in fact knew nothing but what she wrote about him in the two parts of *Tribute to Freud*, until in 1957 I could by chance tell her more and send her some of his books. He was the author of the

---

*The quotation from the letter from Pound to H.D. © 1974 by the Estate of Ezra Pound.

often reprinted *Gods in Exile*, of *The Fire of Creation, The Conquest of Illusion*, and of *The Dramatic History of the Christian Faith*. Born in 1893, he joined the Theosophical Society in 1914, and was General Secretary of the Netherlands Section in 1930–1931. He founded the Practical Idealist Association for youth, and was field organizer for the New Education Fellowship. He lived for a short while in Australia. Of how he reached the Berggasse there is no published record. Looking back, H.D. always remembered him there. 'I wrote of J.J. van der Leeuw and the illness or breakdown I had after I heard of his death in 1933. I connected him with my older brother and the fact that I could not "take" the fact of his death in action in France, because I was expecting this child – so later, with my father's death. Death is all around us.'

'Death and Birth – the great experiences,' as H.D. described them. Emily Dickinson talks much about death. H.D. talks much about both – and about re-birth. Emily Dickinson was wonderfully feminine; H.D. was womanly. One senses the fullness of her experiences, in *Tribute to Freud*, precisely as one feels the skilled warmth of Freud's response. She would remember a person or a phrase and exhibit it to Freud, as he in turn picked up the correlative artifact and symbol from his desk. 'There,' she wrote in 1955 in Küsnacht, still remembering, 'in the print tacked to my wall above the couch, piled high with its heaps of books, manuscripts and letters, sits the Professor at his desk. There are books behind him and books and papers on his desk. There on his desk, too, are a number of the images he so loved and treasured, perhaps (although I do not identify it) the very Egyptian Osiris that he once put into my hands. "This is called the answerer," he said, "because Osiris answers questions." '

Writing on the wall posed questions. Osiris, with the help of Freud, showed the way to answers. It is as H.D. put it in her

Tribute – 'The picture-writing, the hieroglyph of the dream, was the common property of the whole race; in the dream, man, as at the beginning of time, spoke a universal language, and man, meeting in the universal understanding of the unconscious or the subconscious, would forgo barriers of time and space; and man, understanding man, would save mankind.' Man would, could at least, write.

NORMAN HOLMES PEARSON

New Haven, Connecticut

July 1973

A NOTE ON THE TEXT

'Writing on the Wall,' to Sigmund Freud, blameless physician, was written in London in the autumn of 1944, with no reference to the Vienna notebooks of spring 1933.

'Writing on the Wall' appeared in *Life & Letters Today*, London, 1945 – 1946.

'Advent,' the continuation of 'Writing on the Wall,' or its prelude was taken direct from the old notebooks of 1933, though it was not assembled until December 1948, Lausanne.

H.D.

WRITING ON THE WALL

TO SIGMUND FREUD
blameless physician

WRITING ON THE WALL

1

IT WAS VIENNA, 1933–1934. I had a room in the Hotel Regina, Freiheitsplatz. I had a small calendar on my table. I counted the days and marked them off, calculating the weeks. My sessions were limited, time went so quickly. As I stopped to leave my key at the desk, the hall porter said, 'Some day, will you remember me to the Professor?' I said I would if the opportunity arose. He said, '–and ah, the Frau Professor! There is a wonderful lady.' I said I had not met the Frau Professor but had heard that she was the perfect wife for him and there couldn't be – could there? – a greater possible compliment. The porter said, 'You know Berggasse? After the – well, later when the Professor is no longer with us, they will name it Freudgasse.' I went down Berggasse, turned in the familiar entrance; *Berggasse 19, Wien IX,* it was. There were wide stone steps and a balustrade. Sometimes I met someone else coming down.

The stone staircase was curved. There were two doors on the landing. The one to the right was the Professor's professional door; the one to the left, the Freud family door. Apparently, the two apartments had been arranged so that there should be as little confusion as possible between family and patients or students; there was the Professor who belonged to us, there was the Professor who belonged to the family; it was a large family with ramifications, in-laws, distant relatives, family friends. There were other apartments above but I did not very often pass anyone on the stairs, except the analysand whose hour preceded mine.

My hours or sessions had been arranged for me, four days a week from five to six; one day, from twelve to one. At least, that was the arrangement for the second series of sessions which, I have noted, began the end of October 1934. I left a number of books and letters in Switzerland when I left there, actually after the war had begun; among them was my 1933 Vienna diary. I am under the impression that the Professor had arranged the second series to accord with the first, as I had often said to him that that near-evening hour was almost my favorite of the whole day. Anyhow, I had five weeks then. The last session was December 1, 1934. The first series began in March 1933 and lasted somewhat longer, between three and four months. I had not planned on coming back to Vienna, but a great deal had happened between the summer of 1933 and the autumn of 1934. I had heard the news of the Dollfuss affair with some anxiety, but that had not caused any personal repercussions. I came back to Vienna because I heard about the man I sometimes met, coming down the stairs. He had been lecturing at a conference in Johannesburg. He flew his own plane there. On the way back, he crashed in Tanganyika.

2

I DID NOT always pass him on the stairs. He might be lingering on, prolonging his talk in the Professor's study or consulting room, in which case, after hanging up my coat in the hall, I might miss him. I would be ushered direct into the waiting room. Or it might happen that my predecessor emerged from the Professor's sanctum at the same time that I was about to enter. He would be reaching for his coat or his hat while I was disposing of mine. He was very tall, he looked English – yet

English with a catch. He had, it later appeared, spent some time at Oxford, before or after receiving his Continental degree – in any case, he was not German, not American; but how does one know these things? He was, as it happened, exactly what I thought him, 'English with a catch,' in fact, a Dutchman.

I did not know that his name was J. J. van der Leeuw until afterwards. Once he spoke to me at the Professor's bidding, about exchanging hours. That was a summer day in the big house outside the town, at Döbling, where the family moved for the hot months. It would have been a day late in June or early July 1933. The arrangement for receiving us there was more informal, and one did not have quite the same sense of authenticity or *reality* as in the Professor's own home. However, I did not say good-bye to Vienna in the house of a stranger on its outskirts. I came back.

I told the Professor why I had come back. The Professor was seventy-seven at the time of our first sessions. I was forty-seven. Dr. van der Leeuw was considerably younger. He was known among them, the Professor told me, as the Flying Dutchman. He was an eminent scholar. He had come officially to study with the Professor with the idea of the application of the principles of psychoanalysis to general education, with the greater practical aim of international cooperation and understanding. He was wealthy, influential, well-born. He owned vast plantations in the Dutch East Indies and had traveled in India for the purpose of occult investigation. He had contacted a teacher or young devotee there, had been influenced by the Eastern teaching, but that had not satisfied him. He wanted to apply the laws of spiritual being to the acute problems of today. It seemed to me that he was the perfect man for the perfect job. The Professor had not told me that J. J. van der Leeuw was himself aware of a deeply rooted desire or subconscious tendency connected with his brilliant aviation. The Flying Dutchman knew that at any given moment, in the air – his element – he was likely to fly too high, to fly too quickly. 'That was really what concerned me,' said the Professor. 'I can tell you now that that was really what concerned us both.' The Professor added, 'After he left, last time, I felt I had found the solution, I really had the answer. But it was too late.'

I said to the Professor, 'I always had a feeling of satisfaction, of security when I passed Dr. van der Leeuw on the stairs or saw him in the hall. He seemed so self-sufficient, so poised – and you had told me about his work. I felt all the time that he was the person who would apply, carry on the torch – carry on your ideas, but not in a stereotyped way. I felt that you and your work and the future of your work were especially bequeathed to him. Oh, I know there is the great body of the Psycho-Analytical Association, research workers, doctors, trained analysts, and so on! But Dr. van der Leeuw was different. I know that you have felt this very deeply. I came back to Vienna to tell you how sorry I am.'

The Professor said, 'You have come to take his place.'

3

I DID NOT consciously think about the Flying Dutchman or connect him with my own work or weave him into my reveries. My own problems, my own intense, dynamic interest in the unfolding of the unconscious or the subconscious pattern, did not seem to include him. He was so personable, so presentable, apparently so richly intellectually and materially endowed. I envied him, I think, his apparently uncomplicated personality. He was an intellectual type but externalized, the diplomatic or even business type; one did not think of him as tortured or troubled; there seemed nothing of *Sturm und Drang* about him. He appeared scholarly, yes, but not in a bookish introverted sense. You would have said that his body fitted him as perfectly and as suavely as the grey or blue cloth that covered it; his soul fitted his body, you would have said, and his mind fitted his brain or his head; the forehead was high, unfurrowed; his eyes looked perceptive with a mariner's blue gaze, the eyes were a shade off or a shade above blue-grey yet with that grey North Sea in them. Yes – cool, cold, perceptive yet untroubled, you would have said. When later I came to think of it, yes, then it did seem that he was mercurial, Mercury.

I do not think that the name of the winged messenger, Hermes of the Greeks, Mercury of the Romans, ever came up in my talks with the Professor, except once in a roundabout way when I had a dream sequence that included a figure from the famous Raphael Donner fountain in the Marktplatz. This is a very beautiful fountain with reclining figures of river gods, two women and two men. My dream was connected with a young man of my acquaintance in London; his name is not Brooks but his name does suggest streams and rivers so we may call him Brooks. I connected this young Mr. Brooks with the figure of the younger of the male river gods in my dream sequence. It was then that I said to the Professor that the reclining bronze fountain figure had certain affinities with the poised Bolognese Mercury. We agreed that the Raphael Donner figure was the more attractive and original of the two, but that if you should raise the reclining river god and stand him on his feet, he might faintly resemble the Mercury – or in reverse, set the Mercury down to lean on his elbow and he might almost take the place of the bronze fountain figure. It was in any case our Professor's charming way to fall in with an idea, to do it justice but not to overstress unimportant details. For this seemed unimportant at the time.

Perhaps it is not very important now. It is interesting, however, to note in retrospect how the mind hedges away. I connected the Raphael Donner figure, and by implication the Mercury, with a charming but not very important young London acquaintance, while the actual personable image is there in Vienna and was there – had been there – reclining on this very couch, every hour just before my own session. As I say, I did not consciously think about Dr. van der Leeuw or weave him into my reveries. Nor did I think of him as Mercury, the Messenger of the Gods and the Leader of the Dead, after he crashed.

He was a stranger. I did not really know him. We had spoken once in the house at Döbling, outside Vienna. The Professor waved him across the large, unfamiliar drawing room. Dr. van der Leeuw bowed, he addressed me in polite, distinguished German, would the *gnädige Frau* object to altering her hour for one day, tomorrow? I answered him in English, I would not mind at all, I would come at four, he at five. He thanked me pleasantly in friendly English, without a trace of accent. That was the first and last time I spoke to the Flying Dutchman. We had exchanged 'hours.'

4

THE PROFESSOR WAS seventy-seven. His birthday in May was significant. The consulting room in the strange house contained some of his treasures and his famous desk. The room looked the same, except for the desk. Instead of the semicircle of priceless little *objets d'art,* there was a carefully arranged series of vases; each contained a spray of orchids or a single flower. I had nothing for the Professor. I said, 'I am sorry, I haven't brought you anything because I couldn't find what I wanted.' I said, 'Anyway, I wanted to give you something different.' My remark might have seemed a shade careless, a shade arrogant. It might have seemed either of these things, or both. I do not know how the Professor translated it. He waved me to the couch, satisfied or unsatisfied with my apparently casual regard for his birthday.

I had not found what I wanted so I did not give him anything. In one of our talks in the old room at Berggasse, we had gone off on one of our journeys. Sometimes the Professor knew actually my terrain, sometimes it was implicit in a statue or a picture, like that old-fashioned steel engraving of the Temple at Karnak that hung above the couch. I had visited that particular temple, he had not. But this time it was Italy; we were together in Rome. The years went forward, then backward. The shuttle of the years ran a thread that wove my pattern into the Professor's. 'Ah, the Spanish Steps,' said the Professor. 'It was those branches of almond,' I said; 'of all the flowers and the flower baskets, I remember those best.' 'But,' said the Professor, 'the gardenias! In Rome, even *I* could afford to wear a gardenia.' It was not that he conjured up the past and invoked the future. It was a present that was in the past or a past that was in the future.

Even I could search Vienna for a single gardenia or a cluster of gardenias. But I could not find them. Another year, I wrote from London, asking a friend in Vienna – an English student there – to make a special effort to find a cluster of gardenias for the Professor's birthday. She wrote back, 'I looked everywhere for the gardenias. But the florists told me that Professor Freud liked orchids and that people always ordered orchids for his birthday; they thought you would like to know. I sent the orchids for you.'

5

IT WAS SOMETIME later that the Professor received my gardenias. It was not a birthday, it was not Vienna. I had been to see him in London, in new surroundings. He had arrived lately, an exile. It was a large house with a garden. There had been much discussion and anxiety concerning the Professor's famous collection of Greek and Egyptian antiquities and the various Chinese and other Oriental treasures. The boxes had at last arrived, although the family expressed some doubt as to whether or not the entire treasure-trove, or even any of it, would be found intact. At least, the boxes had come, due to the influence and generosity of the Professor's friend and disciple, Madame Marie Bonaparte, the Princess George of Greece; 'the Princess' or 'our Princess,' the Professor called her. I had expressed surprise at seeing several Greek figures on his desk. It seemed to be the same desk in a room that suggested that summer room in the house outside Vienna of my first visit in 1933. But this was autumn 1938. 'How did you manage to bring those from Vienna?' I asked him. 'I did not bring them,' he said. 'The Princess had them waiting for me in Paris, so that I should feel at home there.' It was a treacherous, evil world but there was yet loyalty and beauty in it. It had been a flying, frightening journey. He had told me, five years before in Vienna, that traveling was even then out of the question for him. It was distinctly forbidden him by the distinguished specialist who was always within beck and call. (If I am not mistaken, this devoted friend accompanied the Professor on his journey across the Continent.) It was difficult, seeing the familiar desk, the familiar new-old images on the desk there, to realize that this was London. Indeed, it was better to think of it in terms of a temporary slightly familiar dwelling, as that summer house at Döbling. This pleasant district was geographically, in a sense, to London, what Döbling had been to Vienna. But there was no return to Berggasse, Freudgasse that was to have been.

6

But in imagination at least, in the mist of a late afternoon, I could still continue a quest, a search. There might be gardenias somewhere. I found them in a West End florist's and scribbled on a card, 'To greet the return of the Gods.' The gardenias reached the Professor. I have his letter.

> 20 Maresfield Gardens,
> London, N. W. 3
> Nov. 28th, 1938

Dear H.D.,

I got today some flowers. By chance or intention they are my favourite flowers, those I most admire. Some words 'to greet the return of the Gods' (other people read: Goods). No name. I suspect you to be responsible for the gift. If I have guessed right don't answer but accept my hearty thanks for so charming a gesture. In any case,

> *affectionately yours,*
> *Sigm. Freud*

7

I only saw the Professor once more. It was summer again. French windows opened on a pleasant stretch of lawn. The Gods or the Goods were suitably arranged on ordered shelves.

I was not alone with the Professor. He sat quiet, a little wistful it seemed, withdrawn. I was afraid then, as I had often been afraid, of impinging, disturbing his detachment, of draining his vitality. I had no choice in the matter, anyway. There were others present and the conversation was carried on in an ordered, conventional manner. Like the Gods or the Goods, we were seated in a pleasant circle; a conventionally correct yet superficially sustained ordered hospitality prevailed. There was a sense of outer security, at least no words were spoken to recall a devastatingly near past or to evoke an equivocal future. I was in Switzerland when soon after the announcement of a World at War the official London news bulletin announced that Dr. Sigmund Freud, who had opened up the field of the knowledge of the unconscious mind, the innovator or founder of the science of psychoanalysis, was dead.

8

I HAD ORIGINALLY written *had gone,* but I crossed it out deliberately. Yes, he was dead. I was not emotionally involved. The Professor was an old man. He was eighty-three. The war was on us. I did not grieve for the Professor or think of him. He was spared so much. He had confined his researches to the living texture of wholesome as well as unwholesome thought, but contemporary thought, you might say. That is to say, he had brought the past into the present with his *the childhood of the individual is the childhood of the race* – or is it the other way round? – *the childhood of the race is the childhood of the individual.* In any case (whether or not, the converse also is true), he had opened up, among others, that particular field of the unconscious mind that went to prove that the traits and tendencies of obscure aboriginal tribes, as well as the shape and substance of the rituals of vanished civilizations, were still inherent in the human mind – the human psyche, if you will. But according to his theories the soul existed explicitly, or showed its form and shape in and through the medium of the mind, and the body, as affected by the mind's ecstasies or disorders. About the greater transcendental issues, we never argued. But there was an argument implicit in our very bones. We had come together in order to substantiate something. I did not know what. There was something that was beating in my brain; I do not say my heart – my brain. I wanted it to be let out. I wanted to free myself of repetitive thoughts and experiences – my own and those of many of my contemporaries. I did not specifically realize just what it was I wanted, but I knew that I, like most of the people I knew, in England, America, and on the Continent of Europe, was drifting. We were drifting. Where? I did not know but at least I accepted the fact that we *were* drifting. At least, I knew this – I would (before the current of inevitable events swept me right into the main stream and so on to the cataract) stand aside, if I could (if it were not already too late), and take stock of my possessions. You might say that I had – yes, I had something that I specifically owned. I *owned* myself. I did not really, of course. My family, my friends, and my circumstances owned me. But I *had* something. Say it was a narrow birch-bark canoe. The great forest of the unknown, the supernormal or supernatural, was all around and about us. With the current gathering force, I could at least pull in to the shallows before it was too late, take stock of my very modest possessions of mind and body, and ask the old Hermit who lived on the edge of this vast domain to talk to me, to tell me, if he would, how best to steer my course.

We touched lightly on some of the more abstruse transcendental problems, it is true, but we related them to the familiar family-complex. Tendencies of thought and imagination, however, were not cut away, were not pruned even. My imagination wandered at will; my dreams were revealing, and many of them drew on classical or Biblical symbolism. Thoughts were things, to be collected, collated, analyzed, shelved, or resolved. Fragmentary ideas, apparently unrelated, were often found to be part of a special layer or stratum of thought and memory, therefore to belong together; these were sometimes skillfully pieced together like the exquisite Greek tear-jars and iridescent glass bowls and vases that gleamed in the dusk from the shelves of the cabinet that faced me where I stretched, propped up on the couch in the room in Berggasse 19, Wien IX. The dead were living in so far as they lived in memory or were recalled in dream.

9

In any case, affectionately yours . . . I did not know what enraged him suddenly. I veered round off the couch, my feet on the floor. I do not know exactly what I had said. I have certain notes that I jotted down while in Vienna, but I never worked them over and have barely glanced at them since. I do not want to become involved in the strictly historical sequence. I wish to recall the impressions, or rather I wish the impressions to recall me. Let the impressions come in their own way, make their own sequence. 'There will be plenty of memoirs about the Professor,' Walter Schmideberg said to me. 'I expect Sachs and the Princess have already done theirs.'

The analyst Schmideberg spoke ironically; he was a young Austrian officer on the Russian front, in the First World War, a 'captain of horses' as he described himself to me in the earlier days before his English had become so set. 'Captain of horses' conveyed more to me than 'cavalry officer' or 'officer of the guards'; just as 'needle-tree,' to which he referred one day, than 'pine' or even 'evergreen.' So the impact of a language, as well as the impact of an impression may become 'correct,' become 'stylized,' lose its living quality. It is easy to be caught, like Schmideberg, in the noose of self-criticism, it is easy to say, 'Everybody will be scribbling memoirs,' but the answer to that is, 'Indeed yes, but neither the Princess George of Greece nor Dr. Hanns Sachs aforetime of Vienna and Berlin, later of Boston, Massachusetts, can scribble exactly *my* impressions of the Professor.' Moreover, I don't think anyone could give us a more tender, humorous account of the Professor (if he would let the impressions carry him out of himself) than the former young Rittmeister Schmideberg, who became the world's adept at smuggling cigars to Berggasse during the darkest days of that war, and with whom the Professor kept faith during his bitter year of confinement in an Italian prison-camp, ironically after the war had ended.

10

So much for the Princess, Hanns Sachs, and Walter Schmideberg, the one-time Rittmeister of the 15th Imperial Austro-Hungarian Hussars of His Royal Highness, Archduke Francis Salvator. For myself, I veer round, uncanonically seated stark upright with my feet on the floor. The Professor himself is uncanonical enough; he is beating with his hand, with his fist, on the head-piece of the old-fashioned horsehair sofa that had heard more secrets than the confession box of any popular Roman Catholic father-confessor in his heyday.

This was the homely historical instrument of the original scheme of psychotherapy, of psychoanalysis, the science of the unravelling of the tangled skeins of the unconscious mind and the healing implicit in the process. *Consciously,* I was not aware of having said anything that might account for the Professor's outburst. And even as I veered around, facing him, my mind was detached enough to wonder if this was some idea of *his* for speeding up the analytic content or redirecting the flow of associated images. The Professor said, 'The trouble is – I am an old man *– you do not think it worth your while to love me.'*

11

THE IMPACT of his words was too dreadful – I simply felt nothing at all. I said nothing. What did he expect me to say? Exactly it was as if the Supreme Being had hammered with his fist on the back of the couch where I had been lying. Why, anyway, did he do that? He must know everything or he didn't know anything. He must know what I felt. Maybe he did, maybe that was what this was all about. Maybe, anyway, it was just a trick, something to shock me, to break something in myself of which I was partially aware – something that would not, must not be broken. I was here because I must not be broken. If I were broken, I could not go on here with the Professor. Did he think it was easy to leave friendly, comfortable surroundings and come to a strange city, to beard him, himself, the dragon, in his very den? Vienna? Venice? My mother had come here on her honeymoon, tired, having 'done' Italy as a bride. Maybe my mother was already sheltering the child, a girl, that first child that lived such a very short time. It was the bread she talked of, Vienna and how she loved the different rolls and the shapes of them and ones with

poppy-seeds and Oh – the coffee! Why had I come to Vienna?
The Professor had said in the very beginning that I had come
to Vienna hoping to find my mother. Mother? Mamma. But
my mother was dead. I was dead; that is, the child in me that
had called her mamma was dead. Anyhow, he was a terribly
frightening old man, too old and too detached, too wise and
too famous altogether, to beat that way with his fist, like a
child hammering a porridge-spoon on the table.

I slid back onto the couch. You might say I sneaked back.
With due deliberation and the utmost savoir-faire, I re-
arranged the rug that had slid to the floor. The couch was slip-
pery, the head-piece at the back was hard. I was almost too
long; if I were a little longer my feet would touch the old-fashioned porcelain stove that stood edge-wise in the corner. *The
Nürnberg Stove* was a book that my mother had liked. I could
not remember a single incident of the book and would not
take the time to go through all the intricacies of explaining to
the Professor that I was thinking of a book called *The Nürnberg
Stove*. It was all very obvious; there was the stove, throwing out
its pleasantly perceptible glow, there was the stove itself in the
corner. I saw the porcelain stove and I thought of a book called
The Nürnberg Stove, but why take up time going into all that,
anyway?

There was the stove, but there were moments when one felt
a little chilly. I smoothed the folds of the rug, I glanced surrep-
titiously at my wristwatch. The other day the Professor had
reproached me for jerking out my arm and looking at my
watch. He had said, 'I keep an eye on the time – I will tell you
when the session is over. You need not keep looking at the
time, as if you were in a hurry to get away.' I fingered the strap
of my watch, I tucked my cold hands under the rug. I always
found the rug carefully folded at the foot of the couch when I
came in. Did the little maid Paula come in from the hall and
fold the rug or did the preceding analysand fold it, as I always

carefully did before leaving? I was preceded by the Flying Dutchman; he probably left the rug just anyhow – a man would. Should I ask the Professor if everybody folded the rug on leaving, or if only I did this? The Professor had said in the beginning that he classed me in the same category as the Flying Dutchman – we were students. I was a student, working under the direction of the greatest mind of this and of perhaps many succeeding generations. But the Professor was not always right.

12

I DID NOT argue with the Professor. In fact, as I say, I did not have the answer. If he expected to rouse me to some protestation of affection, he did not then succeed in doing so – the root or the current ran too deep. One day he said, *'Today we have tunneled very deep.'* One day he said, 'I struck oil. It was I who struck oil. But the contents of the oil wells have only just been sampled. There is oil enough, material enough for research and exploitation, to last fifty years, to last one hundred years – or longer.' He said, 'My discoveries are not primarily a heal-all. My discoveries are a basis for a very grave philosophy. There are very few who understand this, *there are very few who are capable of understanding this.'* One day he said to me, 'You discovered for yourself what I discovered for the race.' To all that, I will hope to return later. At the moment, I am lying on the couch. I have just readjusted the rug that had slipped to the floor. I have tucked my hands under the rug. I am wondering if the Professor caught me looking at my wristwatch. I am really somewhat shattered. But there is no answering flareback.

13

THERE IS the old-fashioned porcelain stove at the foot of the couch. My father had a stove of that sort in the outdoor office or study he had had built in the garden of my first home. There was a couch there, too, and a rug folded at the foot. It too had a slightly elevated head-piece. My father's study was lined with books, as this room was. There was a smell of leather, the crackling of wood in the stove, as here. There was one picture, a photograph of Rembrandt's Dissection, and a skull on the top of my father's highest set of shelves. There was a white owl under a bell-jar. I could sit on the floor with a doll or a folder of paper dolls, but I must not speak to him when he was writing at his table. What he was 'writing' was rows and rows of numbers, but I could then scarcely distinguish the shape of a number from a letter, or know which was which. I must not speak to my father when he lay stretched out on the couch, because he worked at night and so must not be disturbed when he lay down on the couch and closed his eyes by day. But now it is I who am lying on the couch in the room lined with books.

But no, there are not many books in this room; it is the other room that is lined with books. The window in this room and the one in the other room look out on to a courtyard, I believe. I am not sure of this. It is quiet here, anyway. There is no sound of traffic from the street, no familiar household sounds as from the Freud-family side of the house. We are quite alone here in this room. But there are two rooms really, though the room beyond is almost part of this room with the wide-parted double doors. There is dusk and darkness beyond, through the parted double doors to the right of the stove, as I lie here.

There is the door across the room that opens in from the little waiting room. There is the other door, at right angles, the exit door. It leads through a rather dark passage or a little room that suggests a pantry or laboratory. Then there is the hall beyond it, where we hang our coats on pegs that somehow suggest school or college. The Flying Dutchman has been and gone. Not only are we alike in our relation to the Professor, as seekers or 'students' as he calls us, but we bear the same relation to the couch that I am lying on. When, in the beginning, I expressed a slight embarrassment at being 'almost too tall,' the Professor put me at ease by saying that the analysand who preceded me was 'actually considerably taller.'

14

MY BROTHER is considerably taller. I am five and he is seven, or I am three and he is five. It is summer. The grass is somewhat dry, a few leaves crackle under our feet. They have fallen from a pear tree that has large russet pears. The pears have been gathered. (*Pears? Pairs?*) There is a tree opposite this, that has small yellow pears; they ripen earlier. The tree next our tree is a crab-apple tree and there is a slice of a large log under it. The log is like a round table or a solid thick stool. It is too heavy for us to move, but Eric, our half-brother (a grown man to us), shifted it easily. We saw what was under the heavy immovable log. There was a variety of entertaining exhibits; small things like ants moved very quickly; they raced frantically around but always returned to the same ridge of damp earth or tiny lump of loam. In neatly sliced runnels, some white, wingless creatures lay curled. The base of the log had been the roof of a series of little pockets or neat open graves, rather like Aztec or Egyptian burial-chambers, but I did not know that.

These curled, white slugs were unborn things. They were repulsive enough, like unlanced boils. Or it is possible that they were not essentially repulsive – they might be cocoonless larvae, they might 'hatch' sometime. But I only saw them, I did not know what they were or what they might portend. My brother and I stood spellbound before this disclosure. Eric watched the frantic circling of the ants attentively. Then he set the log back carefully, so as to crush as few of the beasts as possible, so as to restore, if possible, the protective roof over the heads of the white slugs.

There were things under things, as well as things inside things.

15

BUT THAT WAS another occasion. This time, I am alone with my brother, who is considerably taller. He had summoned me. He had a strip of newspaper in his hand. He had a magnifying glass that he must actually have taken from our father's table. He told me to look and I saw the print on the flimsy news-sheet grown larger, but I knew the glass did this. I did not know why he had to show me this news-print. I did not read. If he wanted to show me something, it should be something more attractive, more suitable altogether. 'Don't go away,' he said, 'it will happen in a minute.' The sun was hot on our backs. The pear branch cast its late-summer shadow toward the crab-apple tree. *'Now,'* he said. Under the glass, on the paper, a dark spot appeared; almost instantaneously the newspaper burst into flames.

It was inevitable that a tall, bearded figure should appear from the Ark-like door of the outdoor study. The study was not flat on the ground but set on a series of square stone pillar-like foundations. Our father came down the steps. This picture could be found in an old collection of Bible illustrations or thumbed-over discarded reproductions of, say, the early nineteenth-century French painter, David. It is a period piece, certainly. Yet its prototype can be found engraved on Graeco-Roman medallions or outlined against the red or black background of jars or amphorae of the classic Greek period. I have said that from my reclining yet propped-up, somewhat Madame Récamier-like position on the couch, I face the wide-open double door. At the foot of the couch is the stove. Placed next the stove is the cabinet that contains the more delicate glass jars and the variously shaped bottles and Aegean vases. In the wall space, on the other side of the double door, is another case or cabinet of curiosities and antiques; on top of this case there are busts of bearded figures – Euripides? Socrates? Sophocles, certainly. There is the window now as you turn that corner, at right angles to this cabinet, and then another case that contains pottery figures and some more Greek-figure bowls. Then, the door to the waiting room. At right angles again, there is the door that leads through the laboratory-like cupboard-room or alcove, to the hall. These two last doors, the entrance door and the exit door, as I call them, are shut. The wall with the exit door is behind my head, and seated against that wall, tucked into the corner, in the three-sided niche made by the two walls and the back of the couch, is the Professor. He will sit there quietly, like an old owl in a tree. He will say nothing at all or he will lean forward and talk about something that is apparently unrelated to the progression or unfolding of our actual dream-content or thought association. He will shoot out an arm, sometimes somewhat alarmingly, to stress a point. Or he will, always making an 'occasion' of it, get up and say, 'Ah – now – we must celebrate *this*,' and proceed to the elaborate ritual – selecting, lighting –

until finally he seats himself again, while from the niche rises the smoke of burnt incense, the smoldering of his mellow, fragrant cigar.

16

LENGTH, BREADTH, thickness, the shape, the scent, the feel of things. The actuality of the present, its bearing on the past, their bearing on the future. Past, present, future, these three – but there is another time-element, popularly called the fourth-dimensional. The room has four sides. There are four seasons to a year. This fourth dimension, though it appears variously disguised and under different subtitles, described and elaborately tabulated in the Professor's volumes – and still more elaborately detailed in the compilations of his followers, disciples, and pseudo-disciples and imitators – is yet very simple. It is as simple and inevitable in the building of time-sequence as the fourth wall to a room. If we alter our course around this very room where I have been talking with the Professor, and start with the wall to my left, against which the couch is placed, and go counter-clockwise, we may number the Professor's wall with the exit door 2, the wall with the entrance door (the case of pottery images and flat Greek bowls) 3, and the wall opposite the couch 4. This wall actually is largely unwalled, as the space there is left vacant by the wide-open double doors.

The room beyond may appear very dark or there may be broken light and shadow. Or even bodily, one may walk into that room, as the Professor invited me to do one day, to look at the things on his table.

17

ON MY FATHER'S table there were pens and ink-bottles and a metal tray for holding the pens. He used different pens for his different inks, black and red. There was a paper-knife of Chinese or pseudo-Chinese design; a squat figure was the handle; a jar or pot on the grotesque's head held a blade that was the paper-knife, though a fret-work in low relief of leaves and tendrils gave the blade of the paper-knife an added dimension; the paper-knife was a paper-knife, at the same time it was a flat tree or pole with delicate tendrils worked over it or through it. There was an oversize pair of desk-shears, several paper-weights; one of glass showed different pictures reflected in it, if you looked into it in a certain light. It was just glass, it was a paper-weight, but it was a set of prismatic triangles, placed on another set of triangles. When you put it down, it always lay sideways; the peak, where one set of triangles met, pointed to the north pole or the south pole, or might have so pointed. There is the magnifying glass which my brother is still holding in his hand.

18

'BUT YOU KNOW, you children are never to play with matches.' It was one of the unforgivable sins. (*Matches?*) My brother has the answer. The answer is a brave, pert rejoinder, 'But we aren't playing with matches.' He does not give the answer. I stand beside him. My brother is very tall. My head scarcely reaches his shoulder. I have seen the round glass in its metal frame; the straight handle is clasped by a damp, somewhat grubby paw, behind my brother's back. I do not know, he does not know that this, besides being the magnifying glass from our father's table, is a sacred symbol. It is a circle and the stem of the circle, the stalk or support of this flower, is the handle of the glass that my brother is clasping behind his back. This is the sacred *ankh,* the symbol of life in Egypt, but we do not know this – or perhaps our father does know this. He used this very sign, the circle with the supporting straight line, with an added little line, a cross, to indicate the planet Venus. I do not know if our father knows that the *ankh* is the symbol of life and that the sign he often uses at the head of one of his columns of numbers is the same sign. He writes columns and columns of numbers, yet at the top of one column he will sketch in a hieroglyph; it may stand for one of the Houses or Signs of the Zodiac, or it may be a planet simply: Jupiter or Mars or Venus. I did not know this when I stood beside my brother in the garden. I knew it a long time after but I did not understand it. It is only now as I write this that I see how my father possessed sacred symbols, how he, like the Professor, had old, old sacred objects on his study table. But the shape and form of these objects, sanctified by time, were not so identified. They were just a glass paper-weight, just a brass paper-knife or the ordinary magnifying glass that my brother is still holding in his hand.

What will my brother say? He cannot say, 'I brought fire from heaven.' He cannot answer father Zeus in elegant iambics and explain how he, Prometheus, by his wit and daring, by his love of the unknown, by his experimentation with occult, as yet unexplainable forces, has drawn down fire from the sky. It is an actual fact. But my brother has never heard of Prometheus, he doesn't know any Greek. He has taken the magnifying glass from our father's study table and that is, possibly, a sin, second only to playing with matches. My father stamps on the flimsy charred paper. There is the smell of burnt paper and the faint trail of smoke in the still air of a late-summer day of the afternoon of the year (perhaps) 1889 or (perhaps) 1901.

I do not remember what my brother says to my father, what my father in his turn says to my brother. 'You must not do it again' is implicit anyway. But the ordinary words of their common speech are sometimes above my head. I do not always even understand the words my brother uses. He is a big boy and known to be quaint and clever for his age. I am a small girl and small for my age and not very advanced. I am, in a sense, still a foreigner. There are other foreigners; they arrive from time to time, in our own house, in our grandfather's house (which is shared by an aunt and uncle), in the house across the street, in other houses, up and down Church Street. These foreigners know even less than I do of the customs of these people about us – civilized or barbaric people. Things happen that these people try to hide from us; a boy drowns in the river, a workman at the steel mill loses a limb, a foreigner or, as they say sometimes at the back door, 'a little stranger' has arrived somewhat prematurely somewhere. All these mysterious, apparently unrelated events, overheard hiding under the kitchen table, or gathered or inferred, whispering with other inarticulate but nonetheless intuitively gifted fellow-whisperers of one's own age, and sometimes a little older, up and down Church Street, have to do with, or in some way suggest, a doctor.

19

A DOCTOR HAS a bag with strange things in it, steel and knives and scissors. Our father is not a doctor but he has a doctor's

picture or a picture of doctors in his study. He is quiet and
strangely tender when we are ill. He likes to tell people that he
hesitated for a time before deciding on his profession, that
doctors always say he should have been one of them. His voice
is quiet and even and low-pitched. His voice is almost monot-
onously quiet. He never raises his voice. He is never irritable
or angry. I never saw him really angry except two or three
times in my whole life, and those were memorable occasions.
Lying on this couch in the Professor's room, I feel that sometime I must recall and annotate (as it were) my father's anger.
But this is not one of those occasions. My father is not angry
now but, though the sun is shining and the burnt paper smoldering at our feet, there is an icy chill in the air. 'Perhaps,' he
may have said (for our father is a just man), 'I did not actually
forbid you taking the magnifying glass,' for my brother has now
handed it back to him. 'I know that I have told you not to
touch the ink-stand or take away the desk-shears or use the
paste-pot for your paper soldiers. It was understood, I
thought, that you did not disturb *anything* on my table.'

There is frost in the air. I sidle nearer to my brother. I am
implicated, though in no way blamed.

20

THERE IS an earlier occasion and again the sun is shining.
From the cloth dress my mother wears, I think it must be
spring, or it is an Indian-summer day, between seasons at any
rate, for my mother wears a cloth dress without a coat. It is not
summer, for we go into summer clothes as regularly and as
inevitably as people in the tropics. We are subtropic, a town in
Pennsylvania, on the map's parallel, I believe, south of Rome.

Winters are cold, summers are hot, so we have the temperament of Nordics and of southerners both, harmoniously blended and altering key or vibration in strict accordance with the seasons' rules – or not, as may be. It is summer anyway in my mother's face, for she is laughing.

We have been out with her to help her with the shopping or to drop in on one of her many relatives or friends. The town contains scarcely anyone who is not a relative or friend – the 'old town' at any rate; and this is the old town, for we are seated on a slight elevation of the pavement, on the curb-stone as it makes a generous curve off Church Street, under the church and on to the stores and hotel and shopping centers of Main Street – I think it was called Main Street; it should be, anyway.

It seems odd that my mother should be laughing. My brother has defied her. He is seated firm on the curb-stone. He is not going home. As he repeats this solemnly, my mother laughs more. People stop and ask what has happened. My mother tells them and they laugh too. They stand either side of my mother, more people, friends and strangers, all laughing. 'But we're collecting a crowd,' she says, 'we can't stay here, crowding the pavement.' She obtains supporters; strangers and near-strangers repeat her words like a Greek chorus, following the promptings of their leader.

There is a slight, whispered conspiracy. The strangers melt away and my mother, with feigned indifference, strolls off. My brother knows perfectly well that she will relent, she will pretend to go away but she will wait around the corner, and if we don't follow her she will come back. He has told her that he is going away to live by himself, and he has moreover told her that his sister is coming with him. His sister waits anxiously, excited yet motionless, on the curb beside him. In addition to this final ultimatum of my brother's, we were not supposed to sit on the curb-stone. But there we sit, not 'crowding the pavement' but making a little group, design, an image at the cross-roads. It appears variously in Greek tragedies with Greek names and it can be found in your original Grimm's tales or in your nursery translation, called Little-Brother, Little-Sister. One is sometimes the shadow of the other; often one is lost and the one seeks the other, as in the oldest fairy tale of the twin-brother-sister of the Nile Valley. Sometimes they are both boys like the stars Castor and Pollux, sometimes there are more than two. Actually in the case of Castor and Pollux there were four, with Helen and Clytemnestra – the children of a Lady, we are told, and a Swan. They make a group, a con-stellation, they make a groove or a pattern into which or upon which other patterns fit, or are placed unfitted and are cut by circumstance to fit. In any case, it is a common-or-garden pat-tern though sometimes it finds its corresponding shape in heaven. And their mother has walked away. *He* knows that she will come back because he is older and is admittedly his mother's favorite. But *she* does not know this. But though her brain is in a turmoil of anxiety and pride and terror, it has not even occurred to her that she might throw her small weight into the balance of conventional behavior by following her mother and leaving her brother to his fate.

21

THESE PICTURES are so clear. They are like transparencies, set before candles in a dark room. I may or may not have men-tioned these incidents to the Professor. But they were there. Upon the elaborate build-up of past memories, across the intricate network made by the hair-lines that divided one irregular bit of the picture-puzzle from another, there fell inevitably a shadow, a writing-on-the-wall, a curve like a reversed, unfinished *S* and a dot beneath it, a question mark, the shadow of a question – *is this it?* The question mark threatened to shadow the apparently most satisfactory answers. No answer was final. The very answer held something of death, of finality, of Dead Sea fruit. The Professor's explanations were too illuminating, it sometimes seemed; my bat-like thought-wings would beat painfully in that sudden searchlight. Or reversely, other wings (gull or skylark) that seemed about to take me right out of the lower levels of the commonplace would find themselves beating in the confined space of a wicker cage, or useless under the mesh of a bird net. But no – he did not set traps, he did not really fling nets. It was I myself, by my own subconscious volition or unconscious will, who walked or flew into them. I over-stressed or over-compensated; I purposely and painfully dwelt on certain events in the past about which I was none too happy, lest I appear to be dodging the analysis or trying to cheat the recorder of the Book of Life, to deceive the Recording Angel, in fact, in an effort to escape the Day of Judgment. Once when I painfully unravelled a dingy, carelessly woven strip of tapestry of cause and effect and related to him, in over-careful detail, some none-too-happy friendships, he waved it all aside, not bored, not grieved or surprised, but simply a little wistful, I thought, as if we had wasted precious time, or precious hours together, on something that didn't matter. 'But why,' he asked, 'did you worry about all this? Why did you think you had to tell me? *Those two didn't count.* But you felt you wanted to tell your mother.'

All this seemed almost too simple at the time. My mother was dead; things had happened before her death, ordinary as well as incredible things, that I hadn't told her. In some cases, I wanted to spare her worry and pain, as during the period of the First World War when I was in England and she was in America. Then there was her personal bereavement to consider; the death of my father followed closely on the news of the death of my older brother in France. My father, a boy of seventeen, and his older brother had been soldiers in our American Civil War and my father had lost this only brother in that war; he was a mathematician, an astronomer, detached and impartial, a scholar or *savant,* to use the more colorful French word. But the news of the death in action of my brother in France brought on a stroke. My father died, literally, from the shock. The Professor had had shock upon shock. But he had not died.

My father was seventy-four or seventy-five when he died – at any rate, not as old as the Professor was now. My mother had had her seventieth birthday in the early twenties. She stayed with me for some years in London and in Vaud, Switzerland. She went back on a visit to America. I knew that she would die there; she knew it too. But I wanted to avoid thinking about this. I did not want to face this. There are various ways of trying to escape the inevitable. You can go round and round in circles like the ants under that log that Eric pried up for us. Or your psyche, your soul, can curl up and sleep like those white slugs.

22

Those two didn't count. There were two's and two's and two's in my life. There were the two actual brothers (the three of us were born within four years). There were the two half-brothers; there were the two tiny graves of the two sisters (one of those was a half-sister but there were the two or twin-graves).

There were the two houses, ours and our grandparents' in the same street, with the same garden. There were the two Biblical towns in Pennsylvania, Bethlehem where I was born, and Philadelphia, where we moved when I was eight. There were for a time in consciousness two fathers and two mothers, for we thought that Papalie and Mamalie (our mother's parents) were our own 'other' father and mother, which, in fact, they were.

There were two of everybody (except myself) in that first house on Church Street. There were the two brothers who shared the same room; the two half-brothers might turn up at any time, together; there were the two maids who slept in the room over the kitchen; there were my two parents in their room. (There was a later addition to this Noah's Ark, but my last brother arrived after this pattern was fixed in consciousness.)

My father had married two times; so again, there were two wives, though one was dead.

Then in later life, there were two countries, America and England as it happened, separated by a wide gap in consciousness and a very wide stretch of sea.

The sea grows narrower, the gap in consciousness sometimes seems negligible; nevertheless there is a duality, the English-speaking peoples are related, brothers, twins even, but they are not one. So in me, two distinct racial or biological or psychological entities tend to grow nearer or to blend, even, as time heals old breaks in consciousness. My father's second wife was the daughter of a descendant of one of the original groups of the early-eighteenth-century, mystical Protestant order, called the Unitas Fratrum, the Bohemian or Moravian Brotherhood. Our mother's father was part mid-European by race, Polish I believe the country called itself then, when his forefathers left it, though it became German and then fluctuated like the other allied districts back and forth as in the earlier days of the Palatinate struggles. Livonia, Moravia, Bohemia – Count Zinzendorf, the founder of the renewed Bohemian brotherhood, was an Austrian, whose father was exiled or self-exiled to Upper Saxony, because of his Protestant affiliations. The Professor himself was an Austrian, a Moravian actually by birth.

23

MOTHER? FATHER? We have met one of them in the garden of the house on Church Street and we have seen the other further down Church Street, where the pavement makes a generous curve under the church on to the shops. But we are not shopping. We are not calling on anyone, friend or near-friend or near or distant relative. Everyone knows our mother so we are never sure who is related and who is not – well, in a sense everyone is related for there is the church and we all belong together in some very special way, because of our candle service on Christmas Eve which is not like what anyone else has anywhere, except in some places in Europe perhaps. Europe is far away and is a place where our parents went on their honeymoon. It is *she* who matters for she is laughing, not so much at us as with or over us and around us. *She* has bound music folios and loose sheets on the top of our piano. About *her*, there is no question. The trouble is, she knows so many people and they come and interrupt. And besides that, she likes my brother better. If I stay with my brother, become part almost of my brother, perhaps I can get nearer to *her*.

But one can never get near enough, or if one gets near, it is because one has measles or scarlet fever. *If* one could stay near her always, there would be no break in consciousness – but half a loaf is better than no bread and there are things, not altogether negligible, to be said for *him*. He has some mysterious habits, this going out at night and sleeping on the couch in his study by day. As far as that goes, there *is* his study. Provided you do not speak to him when he is sitting at his table, or disturb him when he is lying down, you are free to come and go. It is a quiet place. No one interferes or interrupts. His shelves are full of books, the room is lined with books. There is the skull on the top of the highest bookcase and the white owl under a bell-jar. He has more books even than our grandfather and he has that triangle paper-weight that shows the things in the room repeated and in various dimensions. This, of course, I have not at the time actually put into words, hardly put into thoughts. But here I am, in some special way privileged. It is his daughter to whom he later entrusts the paper-knife; he leaves his uncut magazines and periodicals for her. She knows how to run the paper-knife carefully along under the surface of the double page, and this is especially important as her older brother is not invited to cut the pages. He has, of course, many other things to do. Our mother is a mixture of early Pennsylvania settlers, people from this island, England, and others from middle Europe – he is one thing. He is New England, though he does not live there and was not born there. He comes from those Puritan fathers who wear high peaked hats in the Thanksgiving numbers of magazines. They fought with Indians and burned witches. Their hats were like the hats the doctors wore, in the only picture that was hanging in his study. The original picture was by Rembrandt, if I am not mistaken. The half-naked man on the table was dead so it did not hurt him when the doctors sliced his arm with a knife or a pair of scissors. Is the picture called *A Lesson in Anatomy?*

It does not really matter what the picture is called. It is about doctors. There is a doctor seated at the back of the couch on which I am lying. He is a very famous doctor. He is called Sigmund Freud.

24

WE TRAVEL FAR in thought, in imagination or in the realm of memory. Events happened *as* they happened, not all of them, of course, but here and there a memory or a fragment of a dream-picture is actual, is real, is like a work of art or is a work of art. I have spoken of the two scenes with my brother as remaining set apart, like transparencies in a dark room, set before lighted candles. Those memories, visions, dreams, reveries – or what you will – are different. Their texture is different, the effect they have on mind and body is different. They are healing. They are real. They are as real in their dimension of length, breadth, thickness, as any of the bronze or marble or pottery or clay objects that fill the cases around the walls, that are set in elegant precision in a wide arc on the Professor's table in the other room. But we cannot prove that they are real. We can discriminate as a connoisseur (as the Professor does with his priceless collection here) between the false and the true; a good copy of a rare object is not without value, but we must distinguish between a faithful copy and a spurious imitation; there are certain alloys too that may corrode and corrupt in time, and objects so blighted must be segregated or scrapped; there are priceless broken fragments that are meaningless until we find the other broken bits to match them.

There are trivial, confused dreams and there are real dreams. The trivial dream bears the same relationship to the real as a column of gutter-press news-print to a folio page of a play of Shakespeare. The dreams are as varied as are the books we read, the pictures we look at, or the people we meet. *'O dreams* – we know where you Freudians think your dreams come from!' *Your young men shall see visions, and your old men shall dream dreams.* A great many of them come from the same source as the script or Scripture, the Holy Writ or Word. And there too we read of Joseph, how his brethren scoffed, *Behold this dreamer cometh.*

With the Professor, I discussed a few real dreams, some intermediate dreams that contained real imagery or whose 'hieroglyph' linked with authentic images, and some quaint, trivial, mocking dreams that danced, as it were, like masquerading sweeps and May queens round the Maypole. But the most luminous, the most clearly defined of all the dream-content while I was with the Professor was the dream of the Princess, as we called her.

25

SHE WAS a dark lady. She wore a clear-colored robe, yellow or faint-orange. It was wrapped round her as in one piece, like a sari worn as only a high-caste Indian lady could wear it. But she is not Indian, she is Egyptian. She appears at the top of a long staircase; marble steps lead down to a river. She wears no ornament, no circlet or scepter shows her rank, but anyone would know *this is a Princess.* Down, down the steps she comes. She will not turn back, she will not stop, she will not alter the slow rhythm of her pace. She has nothing in her arms, there is no one with her; there is no extraneous object with her or about her or about the carved steps to denote any symbolic detail or side issue involved. There is no detail. The steps are geometrical, symmetrical and she is as abstract as a lady could be, yet she is a real entity, a real person. I, the dreamer, wait at the foot of the steps. I have no idea who I am or how I got there. There is no before or after, it is a perfect moment in time or out of time. I am concerned about something, however. I wait below the lowest step. There, in the water beside me, is a shallow basket or ark or box or boat. There is, of course, a baby nested in it. The Princess must find the baby. I know that she will find this child. I know that the baby will be protected and sheltered by her and that is all that matters.

We have all seen this picture. I pored over this picture as a child, before I could read, in our illustrated Doré Bible. But the black and white Doré illustration has nothing in common with this, except the subject. The name of this picture is *Moses in the Bulrushes* and the Professor of course knows that. The Professor and I discuss this picture. He asks if it is I, the dreamer, who am the baby in the reed basket? I don't think I am. Do I remember if the picture as I knew it as a child had any other figure? I can't remember. The Professor thinks there is the child Miriam, half concealed in the rushes; do I remember? I half remember. Am I, perhaps, the child Miriam? Or am I, after all, in my fantasy, the baby? Do I wish myself, in the deepest unconscious or subconscious layers of my being, to be the founder of a new religion?

26

ANY AMATEUR dabbler with the theories of psychoanalysis can reconstruct, even from this so-far brief evidence, the motive or material or suppressed or repressed psychic urge that projected this dream-picture. There is the little girl with her doll in her father's study. She has come to her father's study to be alone or to be alone with him. Her brother's interests are more lively and exterior and her brother does not enter readily into her doll-family games. He should be the dolls' father or the dolls' doctor, who is called in occasionally. But this does not interest him. He has soldiers and marbles and likes to race about, outdoors and indoors. Here in our father's study, we must be quiet. A girl-child, a doll, an aloof and silent father form this triangle, this family romance, this trinity which follows the recognized religious pattern: *Father,* aloof, distant, the provider, the protector – but a little un-get-at-able, a little too far away and giant-like in proportion, a little chilly withal; *Mother,* a virgin, the Virgin, that is, an untouched child, adoring, with faith, building a dream, and the dream is symbolized by the third member of the trinity, the *Child,* the doll in her arms.

27

THE DOLL IS the dream or the symbol of the dream of this particular child, as these various Ra, Nut, Hathor, Isis, and Ka figures that are dimly apprehended on their shelves or on the Professor's table in the other room are the dream or the symbol of the dream of other aspiring and adoring souls. The childhood of the individual is the childhood of the race, we have noted, the Professor has written somewhere. The child in me has gone. The child has vanished and yet it is not dead. This contact with the Professor intensifies or projects this dream of a Princess, the river, the steps, the child. The river is an Egyptian river, the Nile; the Princess is an Egyptian lady.

Egypt is present, as I say, actually or by inference or suggestion, in the old-fashioned print or engraving of the Temple at Karnak, hanging on the wall above me, as well as in the dimly outlined egg-shaped Ra or Nut or Ka figures on the Professor's desk in the other room. A Queen or Princess is obvious mother-symbol; moreover, there had been casual references, from time to time, to the Professor's French translator, Madame Marie Bonaparte, 'the Princess' or 'our Princess,' as the Professor calls her.

Perhaps here too, as on the occasion of the Professor's birthday in the house at Döbling, I wanted something different or I wanted to give the Professor something different. Princess George of Greece had been consistently helpful and used her influence in the general interests of the Psycho-Analytical Association. She was 'our Princess' in that, as Marie Bonaparte, she had translated the Professor's difficult German into French and was ready to stand by him now that the Nazi peril was already threatening Vienna. She was 'our Princess' in the world, devoted and influential. But is it possible that I sensed another world, another Princess? Is it possible that I (leaping over every sort of intellectual impediment and obstacle) not wished only, but *knew*, the Professor would be born again?

28

FOR THINGS had happened in my life, pictures, 'real dreams,' actual psychic or occult experiences that were superficially, at least, outside the province of established psychoanalysis. But I am working with the old Professor himself; I want his opinion on a series of events. It is true, I had not discussed these experiences openly, but I had sought help from one or two (to my mind) extremely wise and gifted people in the past and they had not helped me. At least, they had not been able to lay, as it were, the ghost. If the Professor could not do this, I thought, nobody could. I could not get rid of the experience by writing about it. I had tried that. There was no use telling the story, into the air, as it were, repeatedly, like the Ancient Mariner who plucked at the garments of the wedding guest with that skinny hand. My own skinny hand would lay, as it were, the cards on the table – here and now – here with the old Professor. He was more than the world thought him – that I well knew. If he could not 'tell my fortune,' nobody else could. He would not call it telling fortunes – heaven forbid! But we would lead up to the occult phenomena, we would show him how it happened. That, at least, we could do – in part, at any rate. I could say, I did say that I had had a number of severe shocks; the news of the death of my father, following the death in action of my brother in France, came to me when I was alone outside London in the early spring of that bad influenza winter of 1919. I myself was waiting for my second child – I had lost the first in 1915, from shock and repercussions of war news broken to me in a rather brutal fashion.

The second child, for some reason, I knew, must be born. Oh, she would be born, all right, though it was an admitted scientific fact that a waiting mother, stricken with that pneumonia, double pneumonia, would not live. She might live – yes – but then the child would not. They rarely both live, if ever! But there were reasons for us both living, so we did live. At some cost, however! The material and spiritual burden of pulling us out of danger fell upon a young woman whom I had only recently met – anyone who knows me knows who this person is. Her pseudonym is Bryher and we all call her Bryher. If I got well, she would herself see that the baby was protected and cherished and she would take me to a new world, a new life, to the land, spiritually of my predilection, geographically of my dreams. We would go to Greece, it could be arranged. It was arranged, though we two were the first unofficial visitors to Athens after that war. This was spring 1920. This spring of 1920 held for me many unresolved terrors, perils, heartaches, dangers, physical as well as spiritual or intellectual. If I had been a little maladjusted or even mildly deranged, it would have been no small wonder. But of a series of strange experiences, the Professor picked out only one as being dangerous, or hinting of danger or a dangerous tendency or symptom. I do not yet quite see why he picked on the writing-on-the-wall as the danger-signal, and omitted what to my mind were tendencies or events that were equally important or equally 'dangerous.' However, as the Professor picked on the writing-on-the-wall as the most dangerous or the only actually dangerous 'symptom,' we will review it here.

29

THE SERIES of shadow- or of light-pictures I saw projected on the wall of a hotel bedroom in the Ionian island of Corfu, at the end of April 1920, belong in the sense of quality and intensity, of clarity and authenticity, to the same psychic category as the dream of the Princess, the Pharaoh's daughter, coming down the stairs. For myself I consider this sort of dream or projected picture or vision as a sort of halfway state between ordinary dream and the vision of those who, for lack of a more definite term, we must call psychics or clairvoyants. Memories too, like the two I have recorded of my father in the garden and my mother on Church Street, are in a sense super-memories; they are ordinary, 'normal' memories but retained with so vivid a detail that they become almost events out of time, like the Princess dream and the writing-on-the-wall. They are steps in the so-far superficially catalogued or built-up mechanism of supernormal, abnormal (or subnormal) states of mind. Steps? The Princess is coming down the steps from a house or palace or hall, far beyond our human habitation. The steps lead down to a river, the river of life presumably, that river named Nile in Egypt. She is 'our Princess' – that is, she is specifically the Professor's Princess and mine, 'our' personal guardian or inspiration. She is peculiarly 'his' Princess for this is a life-wish, apparently, that I have projected into or unto an image of the Professor's racial, ancestral background. We have talked of his age; his seventy-seven symbolized occult power and mystery to me. I frankly told him this without fear of being snubbed or thought ridiculous or superstitious. It is important to me, that seventy-seven, and I have a seven or will acquire one a few months after his May birthday. Mine is, at the time, a forty-seven, so there is thirty years difference in our ages. But ages? Around us are the old images or 'dolls' of pre-dynastic Egypt, and Moses was perhaps not yet born when that little Ra or Nut or Ka figure on the Professor's desk was first hammered by a forger-priest of Ptah on the banks of the Nile.

30

I AM NO DOUBT impressed, probably not a little envious of that gifted lady, 'our Princess' as the Professor calls her. I, no doubt, unconsciously covet her worldly position, her intellectual endowments, her power of translating the difficult, scholarly, beautiful German of Sigmund Freud into no doubt equally distinguished and beautiful French. I cannot compete with her. Consciously, I do not feel any desire to do so. But unconsciously, I probably wish to be another equal factor or have equal power of benefiting and protecting the Professor. I am also concerned, though I do not openly admit this, about the Professor's attitude to a future life. One day, I was deeply distressed when the Professor spoke to me about his grandchildren – what would become of them? He asked me that, as if the future of his immediate family were the only future to be considered. There was, of course, the perfectly secured future of his own work, his books. But there was a more imminent, a more immediate future to consider. It worried me to feel that he had no idea – it seemed impossible – really no idea that he would 'wake up' when he shed the frail locust-husk of his years, and find himself alive.

31

I DID NOT say this to him. I did not really realize how deeply it concerned me. It was a *fact*, but a fact that I had not personally or concretely resolved. I had accepted as part of my racial, my religious inheritance, the abstract idea of immortality, of the personal soul's existence in some form or other, after it has shed the outworn or outgrown body. The *Chambered Nautilus* of the New England poet, Oliver Wendell Holmes, had been a great favorite of mine as a school girl; I did not think of the poem then, but its meters echo in my head now as I write this. *Till thou at length art free,* the last stanza ends, *Leaving thine outgrown shell by life's unresting sea!* And *Build thee more stately mansions, O my soul* is another line, and with the Professor, I did feel that I had reached the high-water mark of achievement;

I mean, I felt that to meet him at forty-seven, and to be accepted by him as analysand or student, seemed to crown all my other personal contacts and relationships, justify all the spiral-like meanderings of my mind and body. I had come home, in fact. And another poem comes inevitably to prompt me:

> On desperate seas long wont to roam,
>   Thy hyacinth hair, thy classic face,
> Thy Naiad airs, have brought me home
>   To the glory that was Greece
>   And the grandeur that was Rome.

This is, of course, Edgar Allan Poe's much-quoted *Helen,* and my mother's name was Helen.

32

THE PROFESSOR translated the pictures on the wall, or the picture-writing on the wall of a hotel bedroom in Corfu, the Greek Ionian island, that I saw projected there in the spring of 1920, as a desire for union with my mother. I was physically in Greece, in Hellas (Helen). I had come home to the glory that was Greece. Perhaps my trip to Greece, that spring, might have been interpreted as a flight from reality. Perhaps my experiences there might be translated as another flight – from a flight. There were wings anyway. I may say that never before and never since have I had an experience of this kind. I saw a dim shape forming on the wall between the foot of the bed and the wash-stand. It was late afternoon; the wall was a dull, mat ochre. I thought, at first, it was sunlight flickering from the shadows cast from or across the orange trees in full leaf and fruit and flower outside the bedroom window. But I realized instantly that our side of the house was already in early shadow. The pictures on the wall were like colorless transfers or 'calcomanias, as we pretentiously called them as children. The first was head and shoulders, three-quarter face, no marked features, a stencil or stamp of a soldier or airman, but the figure was dim light on shadow, not shadow on light. It was a silhouette cut of light, not shadow, and so impersonal it might have been anyone, of almost any country. And yet there was a distinctly familiar line about the head with the visored cap; immediately it was *somebody*, unidentified indeed, yet suggesting a question – dead brother? lost friend?

Then there was the conventional outline of a goblet or cup, actually suggesting the mystic chalice, but it was the familiar goblet shape we all know, with round base and glass-stem. This chalice is as large as the head of the soldier, or rather it simply takes up the same amount of space, as if they were both formal patterns stamped on picture cards, or even (now that I think of it) on playing cards. I have said, with the Professor, that I would lay my cards on the table. These were those cards; so far, two of them. The third follows at once or I now perceive it. It is a simple design in perspective, at least suggesting perspective after the other two flat patterns. It is a circle or two circles, the base the larger of the two; it is joined by three lines, not flat as I say but in perspective, a simple object to draw, once the idea of tilting the planes to give the idea of space is understood. And this object is so simple yet so homely that I think again, 'It's a shadow thrown.' Actually, it could not have been, as this shadow was, 'light'; but the exact replica of this pattern was set on the upper shelf of the old-fashioned wash-stand, along with toothbrush-mug, soap-dish, and those various oddments. It was exactly the stand for the small spirit-lamp we had with us. (*Spirit-lamp?*) And I know that, if these objects are projected outward from my own brain, this is a neat trick, a shortcut, a pun, a sort of joke. For the three-legged lamp-stand in the miscellaneous clutter on the wash-stand is none other than our old friend, the tripod of classic Delphi. So the tripod, this venerated object of the cult of the sun god, symbol of poetry and prophecy, is linked by association with this most ordinary little metal frame that fits into the small saucepan and is used as a support for it when we boil water for that extra sustaining cup of tea upstairs in our room. The tripod then is linked in thought with something friendly and ordinary, the third or second member of my traveler's set, used as base for the flat spirit-lamp and support for the aluminum container. The tripod now becomes all the more an object to be venerated. At any rate, there it is, the third of my cards on the table.

33

SO FAR, SO GOOD – or so far, so dangerous, so abnormal a 'symptom.' The writing, at least, is consistent. It is composed by the same person, it is drawn or written by the same hand. Whether that hand or person is myself, projecting the images as a sign, a warning or a guiding sign-post from my own subconcious mind, or whether they are projected from outside – they are at least clear enough, abstract and yet at the same time related to images of our ordinary time and space. But here I pause or the hand pauses – it is as if there were a slight question as to the conclusion or direction of the symbols. I mean, it was as if a painter had stepped back from a canvas the better to regard the composition of the picture, or a musician had paused at the music-stand, perhaps for a moment, in doubt as to whether he would continue his theme, or wondering perhaps in a more practical manner if he could himself turn the page on the stand before him without interrupting the flow of the music. That is in myself too – a wonder as to the seemliness, or the safety even, of continuing this experience or this experiment. For my head, although it cannot have taken very long in clock-time for these pictures to form there, is already warning me that this is an unusual dimension, an unusual way to *think,* that my brain or mind may not be equal to the occasion. Perhaps in that sense the Professor was right (actually, he was always right, though we sometimes translated our thoughts into different languages or mediums). But there I am seated on the old-fashioned Victorian sofa in the Greek island hotel bedroom, and here I am reclining on the couch in the Professor's room, telling him this, and here again am I, ten years later, seated at my desk in my own room in London. But there is no clock-time, though we are fastidiously concerned with time and with a formal handling of a subject which has no racial and no time-barriers. Here is this hieroglyph of the unconscious or subconscious of the Professor's discovery and life-study, the hieroglyph actually in operation before our very eyes. But it is no easy matter to sustain this mood, this 'symptom' or this inspiration.

And there I sat and there is my friend Bryher who has brought me to Greece. I can turn now to her, though I do not budge an inch or break the sustained crystal-gazing stare at the wall before me. I say to Bryher, 'There have been pictures here – I thought they were shadows at first, but they are light, not shadow. They are quite simple objects – but of course it's very strange. I can break away from them now, if I want – it's just a matter of concentrating – what do you think? Shall I stop? Shall I go on?' Bryher says without hesitation, 'Go on.'

34

WHILE I WAS speaking to Bryher, there is a sort of pictorial buzzing – I mean, about the base of the tripod, there are small creatures, but these are in black; they move about, in and around the base of the tripod, but they are very small; they are like ants swarming, or very small half-winged insects that have not yet learnt to fly. Fly? They are flies, it seems – but no, they are tiny people, all in black or outlined as in, or with, shadow, in distinction to the figures of the three 'cards' already described. They are not a symbol of themselves, they are simply a sort of dust, a cloud or a swarm of small midges that move back and forth, but on one level, as if walking rather than flying. Even as I consider this new aspect of the writing, I am bothered, annoyed – just as one is when suddenly in a country lane one is beset in the evening light by a sudden swarm of midges. They are not important but it would be a calamity if one of them got stuck in one's eye. There was that sort of feeling; people, people – did they annoy me so? Would they perhaps eventually cloud my vision or, worse still, would one of them get 'stuck in my eye'? They were people, they were annoying – I did not hate people, I did not especially resent any one person. I had known such extraordinarily gifted and charming people. They had made much of me or they had slighted me and yet neither praise nor neglect mattered in the face of the gravest issues – life, death. (I had had my child, I was alive.) And yet, so oddly, I knew that this experience, this writing-on-the-wall before me, could not be shared with them – could not be shared with anyone except the girl who stood so bravely there beside me. This girl had said without hesitation, 'Go on.' It was she really who had the detachment and the integrity of the Pythoness of Delphi. But it was I, battered and disassociated from my American family and my English friends, who was seeing the pictures, who was reading the writing or who was granted the inner vision. Or perhaps in some sense, we were 'seeing' it together, for without her, admittedly, I could not have gone on.

35

YET, ALTHOUGH now assured of her support, my own head is splitting with the ache of concentration. I know that if I let go, lessen the intensity of my stare and shut my eyes or even blink my eyes, to rest them, the pictures will fade out. My curiosity is insatiable. This has never happened to me before, it may never happen again. I am not actually analyzing this as I watch the pictures, but it seems now possible that the mechanism of their projection (from within or from without) had something to do with, or in some way was related to, my feelings for the shrine at Delphi. Actually, we had intended stopping off at Itea; we had come from Athens, by boat through the Corinthian canal and up the Gulf of Corinth. Delphi and the shrine of Helios (Hellas, Helen) had been really the main objective of my journey. Athens came a very close second in affection; however, having left Athens, we were informed when the boat stopped at Itea that it was absolutely impossible for two ladies alone, at that time, to make the then dangerous trip on the winding road to Delphi, that in imagination I saw so clearly tucked away under Parnassus. Bryher and I were forced to content ourselves with a somewhat longer stay than was first planned in the beautiful island of Corfu.

But the idea of Delphi had always touched me very deeply and Bryher and I, back in that winter London of the previous spring – it was a winter London that spring – had talked of the famous sacred way. She herself had visited these places with her father before the 1914 war and I had once said to her, while convalescing from the 1919 illness, 'If I could only feel that I could walk the sacred way to Delphi, I know I would get well.' But no, now that we were so near, we could not go to Delphi. We were going in another direction, Brindisi, Rome, Paris, London. Already our half-packed bags, typewriter, books lay strewn about; we obviously *were* leaving. And we were not leaving Corfu in order to return to Athens, as we had talked of doing when we first landed at Corfu, with the thought of a possible arrangement, after all, with a party from one of the archaeological schools at Athens, from Athens itself, overland to Delphi. Travel was difficult, the country itself in a state of political upheaval; chance hotel acquaintances expressed surprise that two women alone had been allowed to come at all at that time. We were always 'two women alone' or 'two ladies alone,' but we were not alone.

36

THERE HAD BEEN writing-on-walls before, in Biblical, in classic literature. At least, all through time, there had been a tradition of warnings or messages from another world or another state of being. Delphi, specifically, was the shrine of the Prophet and Musician, the inspiration of artists and the patron of physicians. Was not the 'blameless physician,' Asklepios himself, reputed to be Phoebus Apollo's own son? Religion, art, and medicine, through the latter ages, became separated; they grow further apart from day to day. These three working together, to form a new vehicle of expression or a new form of thinking or of living, might be symbolized by the tripod, the third of the images on the wall before me, the third of the 'cards' I threw down, as it were on the table, for the benefit of the old Professor. The tripod, we know, was the symbol of prophecy, prophetic utterance or occult or hidden knowledge; the Priestess or Pythoness of Delphi sat on the tripod while she pronounced her verse couplets, the famous Delphic utterances which it was said could be read two ways.

We can read my writing, the fact that there was writing, in two ways or in more than two ways. We can read or translate it as a suppressed desire for forbidden 'signs and wonders,' breaking bounds, a suppressed desire to be a Prophetess, to be important anyway, megalomania they call it – a hidden desire to 'found a new religion' which the Professor ferreted out in the later Moses picture. Or this writing-on-the-wall is merely an extension of the artist's mind, a *picture* or an illustrated poem, taken out of the actual dream or daydream content and projected from within (though apparently from outside), really a high-powered *idea*, simply over-stressed, *over-thought*, you might say, an echo of an idea, a reflection of a reflection, a 'freak' thought that had got out of hand, gone too far, a 'dangerous symptom.'

37

But symptom or inspiration, the writing continues to write itself or be written. It is admittedly picture-writing, though its symbols can be translated into terms of today; it is Greek in spirit, rather than Egyptian. The original or basic image, however, is common to the whole race and applicable to almost any time.

38

So FAR THE PICTURES, the transfers or "calcomanias,' have run level on the wall space between the foot of the bed and the wash-stand. Now they take an upward course or seem about to do so. The 'buzzing' seems to have ceased or the black flies have flown away or the shadow-people faded out. The first three pictures or 'cards on the table' were static, they were there complete; or dimly there, they became less dim as the outline and the meaning became recognizable. But this picture or symbol begins to draw itself before my eyes. *The moving finger writes.* Two dots of light are placed or appear on the space above the rail of the wash-stand, and a line forms, but so very slowly – as if the two rather heavy dots elongated from their own centers, as if they faded in intensity as two lines emerged, slowly moving toward one another. They will meet, it is evident, and from the pattern (two dots on a blackboard) we will get a single line. I do not know how long it took for these two frail lines to meet and then to remain one, intensified or in italics, underlined as it were. One line? It may have taken a split fraction of a second to form, but now I am perfectly well aware that this concentration is a difficult matter. My facial muscles seem stiff with the effort and I may become frozen like one of those enemies of Athené, the goddess of wisdom, to whom Perseus showed the Gorgon head. Am I looking at the Gorgon head, a suspect, an enemy to be dealt with? Or am I myself Perseus, the hero who is fighting for Truth and Wisdom? But Perseus could find his way about with winged sandals and the cloak of invisibility. Moreover, he himself could wield the ugly weapon of the Gorgon's severed head, because Athené (or was it Hermes, Mercury?) had told him what to do. He was himself to manipulate his weapon, this ugly severed head of the enemy of Wisdom and Beauty, by looking at it in the polished metal of his shield. Even he, the half-god or hero, would be turned to stone, frozen if he regarded too closely and without the shield to protect him, in its new quality of looking-glass or reflector, the ugly Head or Source of evil. So I, though I did not make this parallel at the time, still wondered. But even as I wondered, I kept the steady concentrated gaze at the wall before me.

39

THERE IS ONE LINE clearly drawn, but before I have actually recovered from this, or have had time to take breath, as it were, another two dots appear and I know that another line will form in the same way. So it does, each line is a little shorter than its predecessor, so at last, there it is, this series of foreshortened lines that make a ladder or give the impression of a ladder set up there on the wall above the wash-stand. It is a ladder of light, but even now I may not take time, as I say, to draw breath. I may be breathing naturally but I have the feeling of holding my breath under water. As if I were searching under water for some priceless treasure, and if I bobbed up to the surface the clue to its whereabouts would be lost forever. So I, though seated upright, am in a sense diving, head-down under water – in another element, and as I seem now so near to getting the answer or finding the treasure, I feel that my whole life, my whole being, will be blighted forever if I miss this chance. I must not lose grip, I must not lose the end of the picture and so miss the meaning of the whole, so far painfully perceived. I must hold on here or the picture will blur over and the sequence be lost. In a sense, it seems I am drowning;

already half-drowned to the ordinary dimensions of space and time, I know that I must drown, as it were, completely in order to come out on the other side of things (like Alice with her looking-glass or Perseus with his mirror). I must drown completely and come out on the other side, or rise to the surface after the third time down, not dead to this life but with a new set of values, my treasure dredged from the depth. I must be born again or break utterly.

40

THESE LINES SEEM to take such a long time to form separately. Perhaps they are symbolic ages or aeons. Anyhow, I have been able to concentrate, to hold the picture so far. There are maybe seven rungs to this ladder, maybe five; I did not count them. They are symbolic anyway, the ladder itself is a symbol well authenticated; it is Jacob's ladder if you will; it is a symbol common to all religious myth or lore.

But fortunately the last figure to form does so, quickly; at least, there seems less strain and worry of waiting now. There she is, I call her she; I call her Niké, Victory. She is facing the wall or moving as against the wall up from the last rung of the ladder and she moves or floats swiftly enough. To my right, to her right on the space between the ladder and the mirror-frame above the wash-stand, there is a series of broken curves. Actually, they are above the ladder, not touching the angel who brushes past them. I realize that this decorative detail is in a sense suggested by the scrollwork of the mirror-frame, but as in the case of the tripod (also suggested by, or reminding me of a natural homely object on the stand there), cannot not be a replica of it, a shadow of it, for again the scrollwork is drawn in *light* and would not anyway match a shadow direction even if shadow could be thrown. The *S* or half-*S* faces the angel; that is, the series of the *S*-pattern opens out in the direction of the angel; they are like question marks without the dot beneath them. I did not know what this scrollwork indicated; I thought at the time that it was a mere wave-like decorative detail. But now I think this inverted *S*-pattern may have represented a series of question marks, the questions that have been asked through the ages, that the ages will go on asking.

41

VICTORY, NIKÉ, as I called her exactly then and there, goes on. She is a common-or-garden angel, like any angel you may find on an Easter or Christmas card. Her back is toward me, she is simply outlined but very clearly outlined like the first three symbols or 'cards.' But unlike them, she is not flat or static, she is in space, in unwalled space, not flat against the wall, though she moves upward as against its surface. She is a moving-picture and fortunately she moves swiftly. Not swiftly exactly but with a sure floating that at least gives my mind some rest, as if my mind had now escaped the bars of that ladder, no longer climbing or caged but free and with wings. On she goes. Above her head, to her left in the space left vacant on this black-board (or light-board) or screen, a series of tent-like triangles forms. I say tent-like triangles, for though they are simple triangles they suggest tents to me. I feel that the Niké is about to move into and through the tents, and this she exactly does. So far – so good. But this is enough. I drop my head in my hands; it is aching with this effort of concentration, but I feel that I have seen the picture. I thought, 'Niké, Victory,' and even as I thought it, it seemed to me that this Victory was not now, it was another Victory; in which case there would be another war. When that war had completed itself, rung by rung or year by year, I, personally (I felt), would be free, I myself would go on in another, a winged dimension. For the tents, it seemed to me, were not so much the symbolic tents of the past battlefields, the near past or the far past, but tents or shelters to be set up in another future contest. The picture now seemed to be something to do with another war, but even at that there would be Victory. Niké, Victory seemed to be the clue, seemed to be my own especial sign or part of my hieroglyph. We had visited in Athens, only a short time ago, the tiny Temple of Victory that stands on the rock of the Acropolis, to your right as you turn off from the Propylaea. I must hold on to this one word. I thought, 'Niké, Victory.' I thought, 'Helios, the sun . . .' And I shut off, 'cut out' before the final picture, before (you might say) the explosion took place.

But though I admit to myself that now I have had enough, maybe just a little too much, Bryher, who has been waiting by me, carries on the 'reading' where I left off. Afterwards she told me that she had seen nothing on the wall there, until I dropped my head in my hands. She had been there with me patient, wondering, no doubt deeply concerned and not a little anxious as to the outcome of my state or mood. But as I relaxed, let go, from complete physical and mental exhaustion, she saw what I did not see. It was the last section of the series, or the last concluding symbol – perhaps that 'determinative' that is used in the actual hieroglyph, the picture that contains the whole series of pictures in itself or helps clarify or explain them. In any case, it is apparently a clear enough picture or symbol. She said it was a circle like the sun-disk and a figure within the disk; a man, she thought, was reaching out to draw the image of a woman (my Niké) into the sun beside him.

42

THE YEARS BETWEEN seemed a period of waiting, of marking time. There was a growing feeling of stagnation, of lethargy, clearly evident among many of my own contemporaries. Those who were aware of the trend of political events, on the other hand, were almost too clever, too politically minded, too high-powered intellectually for me altogether. What I seemed to sense and wait for was frowned upon by the first group, though I learned very early not to air my thoughts and fears; they were morbid, they were too self-centered and introspective altogether. Why – my brother-in-law spent such a happy holiday in the Black Forest (with – so-and-so – chapter and verse) and the food was so good – everybody was so hospitable and so very charming. If, on the other hand, I ventured a feeble opinion to the second group, I was given not chapter and verse so much as the whole outpouring of pre-digested voluminous theories. My brain staggers now when I remember the deluge of brilliant talk I was inflicted with; what would happen if, and who would come to power when – but with all their abstract clear-sightedness, this second group seemed as muddled, as lethargic in their own way, as the first. At least, their theories and their accumulated data seemed unrooted, raw. But this, I admit – yes, I know – was partly due to my own hopeless feeling in the face of brilliant statisticians and one-track-minded theories. *Where is this taking you,* I wanted to shout at both parties. One refused to admit the fact that the flood was coming – the other counted the nails and measured the planks with endless exact mathematical formulas, but didn't seem to have the very least idea of how to put the Ark together.

43

ALREADY IN VIENNA, the shadows were lengthening or the tide was rising. The signs of grim coming events, however, manifested in a curious fashion. There were, for instance, occasional coquettish, confetti-like showers from the air, gilded paper swastikas and narrow strips of printed paper like the ones we pulled out of our Christmas bon-bons, those gay favors that we called 'caps' as children in America and that English children call 'crackers.' The party had begun, or this was preliminary to the birthday or the wedding. I stooped to scrape up a handful of these confetti-like tokens as I was leaving the Hotel Regina one morning. They were printed on those familiar little oblongs of thin paper that fell out of the paper cap when it was unfolded at the party; we called them mottoes. These mottoes were short and bright and to the point. One read in clear primer-book German, 'Hitler gives bread,' 'Hitler gives work,' and so on. I wondered if I should enclose this handful in a letter to one of my first group of friends in London – or to one of the second. I had a mischievous picture of this gay shower falling on a carpet in Kensington or Knightsbridge or on a bare floor in a Chelsea or Bloomsbury studio. It would be a good joke. The paper was crisp and clean, the gold clear as Danaë's legendary shower, and the whole savored of birthday cake and candles or fresh-bought Christmas-tree decorations. The gold, however, would not stay bright nor the paper crisp very long, for people passed to and fro across Freiheitsplatz and along the pavement, trampling over this Danaë shower, not taking any notice. Was I the only person in Vienna who had stooped to scrape up a handful of these tokens? It seemed so. One of the hotel porters emerged with a long-handled brush-broom. As I saw him begin methodically sweeping the papers off the pavement, I dropped my handful in the gutter.

44

THERE WERE OTHER swastikas. They were the chalk ones now; I followed them down Berggasse as if they had been chalked on the pavement especially for my benefit. They led to the Professor's door – maybe, they passed on down another street to another door but I did not look any further. No one brushed these swastikas out. It is not so easy to scrub death-head chalk-marks from a pavement. It is not so easy and it is more conspicuous than sweeping tinsel paper into a gutter. And this was a little later.

45

THEN THERE WERE rifles. They were stacked neatly. They stood in bivouac formations at the street corners. It must have been a weekend; I don't remember. I could verify the actual date of their appearance by referring to my notebooks, but it is the general impression that concerns us, rather than the historical or political sequence. They were not German guns – but perhaps they were; anyway, these were Austrian soldiers. The stacks of rifles gave the streets a neat, finished effect, as of an 1860 print. They seemed old-fashioned, the soldiers seemed old-fashioned; I was no doubt reminded of familiar pictures of our American Civil War. This was some sort of civil war. No one would explain it to me. The hall porter, usually so talkative, was embarrassed when I questioned him. Well, I must not involve him in any discussion or dangerous statement of opinion. I went out anyway. There were some people about and the soldiers were out of a picture or a film of a reconstructed Civil War period. They did not seem very formidable. I had meant to go to the opera – it was late afternoon or early evening – so I might as well go to the opera, if there were an opera, as mope in my room or loiter about the hotel, wondering and watching. When challenged on one of the main thoroughfares, I said simply, in my sketchy German, that I was a visitor in Vienna; they called me the English lady at the hotel, so I said I was from England, which in fact I was. What was I doing? Where was I going? I said I was going to the opera, if I was not disturbing them or getting in their way. There was a little whispering and shuffling and I was embarrassed to find that I had attracted the attention of the officers and had almost a guard of honor to the steps of the opera house, where there were more guns and soldiers, seated on the steps and standing at attention on the pavement. It seemed that nothing, at any rate, could stop the opera. I stayed for part of the performance of – I don't remember what it was – and had no trouble finding my way back.

46

THEN IT WAS QUIET and the hotel lobby seemed strangely empty. Even the hall porter disappeared from behind his desk. Maybe this was the following Monday; in any case, I was due at Berggasse for my usual session. The little maid, Paula, peered through a crack in the door, hesitated, then furtively ushered me in. She did not wear her pretty cap and apron. Evidently, she was not expecting me. 'But – but no one has come today; no one has gone out.' All right, would she explain to the Professor, in case he did not want to see me. She opened the waiting-room door. I waited as usual in the room, with the round table, the odds and ends of old papers and magazines. There were the usual framed photographs; among them, Dr. Havelock Ellis and Dr. Hanns Sachs greeted me from the wall. There was the honorary diploma that had been presented to the Professor in his early days by the small New England university. There was also a bizarre print or engraving of some nightmare horror, a 'Buried Alive' or some such thing, done in Düreresque symbolic detail. There were long lace curtains at the window, like a 'room in Vienna' in a play or film.

The Professor opened the inner door after a short interval. Then I sat on the couch. The Professor said, 'But why did you come? No one has come here today, no one. What is it like outside? Why did you come out?'

I said, 'It's very quiet. There doesn't seem to be anyone about in the streets. The hotel seems quiet, too. But otherwise, it's much the same as usual.' He said, 'Why did you come?' It seemed to puzzle him, he did not seem to understand what had brought me.

47

WHAT DID HE expect me to say? I don't think I said it. My being there surely expressed it? *I am here because no one else has come.* As if again, symbolically, I must be different. Where was the Flying Dutchman? Or the American lady-doctor whom I had not seen? There were only four of us at that time, I believe, rather special people. It is true that Mrs. Burlingham, Miss Anna Freud's devoted friend, and the Professor's disciple or pupil, had an apartment, further up the stairs. I had gone up there to tea one day before my session here. The Professor was not really alone. The envoys of the Princess, too, I had been informed, were waiting on the door-steps of various legations and they would inform her of any actual threat to the Professor's personal safety. But, in a sense, I was the only one who had come from the outside; little Paula substantiated that when she peered so fearfully through the crack in the front door. Again, I was different. I had made a unique gesture, although actually I felt my coming was the merest courtesy; this was our usual time of meeting, our session, our 'hour' together. I did not know what the Professor was thinking. He could not be thinking, 'I am an old man – *you do not think it worth your while to love me.*' Or if he remembered having said that, this surely was the answer to it.

48

IT MAY HAVE BEEN that day or another that the Professor spoke of his grandchildren. In any case, whenever it was, I felt a sudden gap, a severance, a chasm or a schism in consciousness, which I tried to conceal from him. It was so tribal, so conventionally Mosaic. As he ran over their names and the names of their parents, one felt the old impatience, a sort of intellectual eye-strain, the old boredom of looking out historical, genealogical references in a small-print school or Sunday-school Bible. It was Genesis but not the very beginning. Not the exciting verses about the birds and the reptiles, the trees, the sun and the moon, those greater and lesser lights. He was worried about them (and no small wonder), but I was worried about something else. I did not then realize the reason for my anxiety. I knew the Professor would move on somewhere else, before so very long, but it seemed the eternal life he visualized was in the old Judaic tradition. He would live forever like Abraham, Isaac, and Jacob, in his children's children, multiplied like the sands of the sea. That is how it seemed to me his mind was working, and that is how, faced with the blank wall of danger, of physical annihilation, his mind would work.

At least, there was that question between us, 'What will become of my grandchildren?' He was looking ahead but his concern for immortality was translated into terms of grandchildren. He would live in them; he would live in his books, of course; I may have murmured something vaguely to the effect that future generations would continue to be grateful to his written word; that, I may have mentioned – I am sure I did sometime or other, on that or another occasion. But though a sincere tribute, those words were, or would be, in a sense, superficial. They would fall flat, somehow. It was so very obvious that his work would live beyond him. To express this adequately would be to delve too deep, to become involved in technicalities, and at the same time it would be translating my admiration for what he stood for, what actually he *was*, into terms a little too formal, too prim and precise, too conventional, too banal, too *polite*.

I did not want to murmur conventional words; plenty of people had done that. If I could not say exactly what I wanted to say, I would not say anything, just as on his seventy-seventh birthday, if I could not find what I wanted to give, I would not give anything. I did find what I wanted, that cluster of gardenias, somewhat later; that offering was in the autumn of 1938. And these words, the words that I could not speak then, too, come somewhat later, in the autumn of 1944. The flowers and the words bear this in common, they are what I want, what I waited to find for the Professor, 'to greet the return of the Gods.' It is true, 'other people read: Goods.' A great many people had read 'goods' and would continue to do so. But the Professor knew, he must have known, that, by implication, he himself was included in the number of those Gods. He himself already counted as immortal.

49

I DID NOT know exactly *who* he was and yet it seems very obvious now. Long ago, in America, I had a peculiar dream or merely a flash of vision. I was not given to these things, though as a small child, in common with many other small children, I had had one or two visionary or supernormal experiences. This time I must have been eighteen or nineteen. The picture or segment of picture impressed me so much that I tried to identify it. It was not a very sensational experience. The vision or picture was simply this: before sleeping or just on wakening, there was a solid shape before my eyes, no luminous cloud-pictures or vague fantasy, but an altar-shaped block of stone; this was divided into two sections by the rough stone marking; it was hardly a carved line but it was definitely a division of the surface of the rough stone into two halves. In one half or section, there was a serpent, roughly carved; he was conventionally coiled with head erect; on the other side, there was a roughly incised, naturalistic yet conventionally drawn thistle. Why this?

It is odd to think, at this very late date, that it was Ezra Pound who helped me interpret this picture. Ezra was a year older; I had known him since I was fifteen. I do not think I spoke of this to anyone but Ezra and a girl, Frances Josepha, with whom later I took my first trip to Europe. Ezra at that time was staying with his parents in a house outside Philadelphia, for the summer months. It was there, one afternoon, that Ezra said, 'I have an idea about your snake on a brick,' as he called it. We went into the study or library – it was a furnished house, taken over from friends – and Ezra began jerking out various reference books and concordances. He seemed

satisfied in the end that this was a flashback in time or a pre-
vision of some future event that had to do with Aesculapius or
Asklepios, the human or half-human, half-divine child of
Phoebus Apollo, who was slain by the thunder-bolt or light-
ning-shaft of Zeus, but later placed among the stars. The serpent is certainly the sign or totem, through the ages, of healing
and of that final healing when we slough off, for the last time,
our encumbering flesh or skin. The serpent is symbol of death,
as we know, but also of resurrection.

There was no picture of this. Ezra said airily, 'The thistle
just goes with it.' I do not think he actually identified the
thistle in connection with the serpent, but in any case it was he
who first gave me the idea of Asklepios, the 'blameless physician,' in that connection. I found this design later but only
once and in only one place. I was with Frances Josepha and
her mother on our first trip 'abroad.' This was the summer of
1911. We went from New York to Havre, then by boat up the
Seine to Paris. 'Here it is,' I said on one of our first visits to the
galleries of the Louvre, 'quick,' as if it might vanish like the
original 'brick.' It was a small signet-ring in a case of Graeco-
Roman or Hellenistic seals and signets. Under the glass, set in
a row with other seal-rings, was a little grey-agate oval. It was
a small ring with rather fragile setting, as far as one could
judge, but the design was unmistakable. On the right side, as
in the original, was the coiled, upright serpent; on the left, an
exquisitely chased stalk, with the spiny double leaf and the
flower-head, our thistle. I have never found this design anywhere else; there are serpents enough and heraldic thistles but
I have not found the two in combination, though I have leafed
over reference books from time to time, at odd moments, or
glanced over classic coin designs or talismans just 'in case.' I
never found my serpent and thistle in any illustrated volume
of Greek or Ptolemaic design or in any odd corner on an actual

Greek pottery jar or Etruscan vase, but through the years as I stopped off in Paris, on cross-continental journeys, I went back to assure myself that I had not, at any rate, 'dreamt' the signet-ring. There it was; it was always in the same place, under the glass, in the frame, with the small slip of faded paper with a letter or a group of letters and a number. Once I even went to the length of purchasing the special catalogue that dealt with this section, hoping for some detail, but there was the briefest mention of 'my' little ring; I read, 'intaglio or signet-ring of Graeco-Roman or Hellenistic design,' and a suitable approximate date. That was all.

50

SIGNET – as from sign, a mark, token, proof; signet – the privy seal, a seal; signet-ring – a ring with a signet or private seal; sign-manual – the royal signature, usually only the initials of the sovereign's name. (I have used my initials H.D. consistently as my writing signet or sign-manual, though it is only, at this very moment, as I check up on the word 'signet' in my Chambers' English Dictionary that I realize that my writing signature has anything remotely suggesting sovereignty or the royal manner.) Sign again – a word, gesture, symbol, or mark, intended to signify something else. Sign again – (medical) a symptom, (astronomical) one of the twelve parts of the Zodiac. Again sign – to attach a signature to, and sign-post – a direction post; all from the French, *signe,* and Latin, *signum.* And as I write that last word, there flashes into my mind the associated *in hoc signum* or rather, it must be *in hoc signo* and *vinces.*

51

THERE WAS A HANDFUL of old rings in a corner of one of the Professor's cases and I thought of my signet-ring at the galleries of the Louvre in Paris, but I did not speak of it to the Professor then or later, and though I felt curious about the rings at the time, I did not suggest his opening the door of the case and showing them to me. He had taken up one of the figures on his desk. He was holding it in his hand and looking at me. This, I surmised, was the image that he thought would interest me most. There was an ivory Indian figure in the center; the objects were arranged symmetrically and I wondered if the seated Vishnu (I think it was) belonged there in the center by right of precedence or preference or because of its shape. Though I realized the beautiful quality and design of the ivory, I was seeing it rather abstractly; the subject itself did not especially appeal to me. Serpent-heads rose like flower petals to form a dome or tent over the head of the seated image; possibly it was seated on a flower or leaf; the effect of the whole was of a half-flower, cut lengthwise, the figure taking the place or producing the effect of a stamen-cluster or oval seed-pod, in the center. Only when you came close, you saw the little image and the symmetrical dome-like background of the snakes' heads. It is true, these snake-heads suggested, each, a half-*S*, which might have recalled the scroll pattern of the inverted *S* or incomplete question mark in the picture series on the wall of the bedroom in the Greek island of Corfu of that spring of 1920. But I did not make this comparison then or afterwards to the Professor, and I felt a little uneasy before the extreme beauty of this carved Indian ivory which compelled me, yet repelled me, at the same time.

I did not always know if the Professor's excursions with me

into the other room were by way of distraction, actual social occasions, or part of his plan. Did he want to find out how I would react to certain ideas embodied in these little statues, or how deeply I felt the dynamic *idea* still implicit in spite of the fact that ages or aeons of time had flown over many of them? Or did he mean simply to imply that he wanted to share his treasures with me, those tangible shapes before us that yet suggested the intangible and vastly more fascinating treasures of his own mind? Whatever his idea, I wanted then, as at other times, to meet him halfway; I wanted to return, in as unobtrusive a way as possible, the courtesy that was so subtly offered me. If it was a *game,* a sort of roundabout way of finding out something that perhaps my unconscious guard or censor was anxious to keep from him, well, I would do my best to play this game, this guessing game – or whatever it was. So, as the ivory had held my attention and perhaps (I did not know) it was especially valued by him, as it held the center place on his imposing desk (that seemed placed there, now I come to think of it, almost like a high altar, in the Holy of Holies), I said, realizing my slight aversion to this exquisite work of art, 'That ivory – what is it? It's Indian obviously. It's very beautiful.'

He said, barely glancing at the lovely object, 'It was sent to me by a group of my Indian students.' He added, 'On the whole, I think my Indian students have reacted in the least satisfactory way to my teaching.' So much for India, so much for his Indian students. This was not his favorite, this Oriental, passionate, yet cold abstraction. He had chosen something else. It was a smallish object, judging by the place left empty, my end of the semicircle, made by the symmetrical arrangement of the Gods (or the Goods) on his table. '*This* is my favorite,' he said. He held the object toward me. I took it in my hand. It was a little bronze statue, helmeted, clothed to the foot in carved robe with the upper incised chiton or peplum.

One hand was extended as if holding a staff or rod. 'She is perfect,' he said, *'only she has lost her spear.'* I did not say anything. He knew that I loved Greece. He knew that I loved Hellas. I stood looking at Pallas Athené, she whose winged attribute was Niké, Victory, or she stood wingless, Niké A-pteros in the old days, in the little temple to your right as you climb the steps to the Propylaea on the Acropolis at Athens. He too had climbed those steps once, he had told me, for the briefest survey of the glory that was Greece. Niké A-pteros, she was called, the Wingless Victory, for Victory could never, would never fly away from Athens.

52

SHE HAS LOST HER SPEAR. He might have been talking Greek. The beautiful tone of his voice had a way of taking an English phrase or sentence out of its context (out of the associated context, you might say, of the whole language) so that, although he was speaking English without a perceptible trace of accent, yet he was speaking a foreign language. The tone of his voice, the singing quality that so subtly permeated the texture of the spoken word, made that spoken word live in another dimension, or take on another color as if he had dipped the grey web of conventionally woven thought and with it, conventionally *spoken* thought, into a vat of his own brewing – or held a strip of that thought, ripped from the monotonous faded and outworn texture of the language itself, into the bubbling cauldron of his own mind in order to draw it forth dyed blue or scarlet, a new color to the old grey mesh, a scrap of thought, even a cast-off rag, that would become hereafter a pennant, a standard, a *sign* again, to indicate a direction or, fluttering aloft on a pole, to lead an army.

And on the other hand, when he said, *she is perfect,* he meant
not only that the little bronze statue was a perfect symbol,
made in man's image (in woman's, as it happened), to be venerated as a projection of abstract thought, Pallas Athené, born
without human or even without divine mother, sprung full-
armed from the head of her father, our-father, Zeus, Theus, or
God; he meant as well, this little piece of metal you hold in
your hand (look at it) is priceless really, it is *perfect,* a prize, a
find of the best period of Greek art, the classic period in its
most concrete expression, before it became top-heavy with
exterior trappings and ornate detail. This is a perfect speci-
men of Greek art, produced at the moment when the archaic
abstraction became humanized but not yet over-humanized.

'She is perfect,' he said and he meant that the image was of
the accepted classic period, Periclean or just pre-Periclean; he
meant that there was no scratch or flaw, no dent in the surface
or stain on the metal, no fold of the peplum worn down or
eroded away. He was speaking as an ardent lover of art and an
art-collector. He was speaking in a double sense, it is true, but
he was speaking of value, the actual intrinsic value of the
piece; like a Jew, he was assessing its worth; the blood of Abraham, Isaac, and Jacob ran in his veins. He knew his material
pound, his pound of flesh, if you will, but this pound of flesh
was a *pound of spirit* between us, something tangible, to be
weighed and measured, to be weighed in the balance and –
pray God – not to be found wanting!

53

HE HAD SAID, he had dared to say that the dream had its worth
and value in translatable terms, not the dream merely of a

Pharaoh or a Pharaoh's butler, not the dream merely of the
favorite child of Israel, not merely Joseph's dream or Jacob's
dream of a symbolic ladder, not the dream only of the
Cumaean Sybil of Italy or the Delphic Priestess of ancient
Greece, but the dream of everyone, everywhere. He had dared
to say that the dream came from an unexplored depth in
man's consciousness and that this unexplored depth ran like a
great stream or ocean underground, and the vast depth of that
ocean was the same vast depth that today, as in Joseph's day,
overflowing in man's small consciousness, produced
inspiration, madness, creative idea, or the dregs of the
dreariest symptoms of mental unrest and disease. He had
dared to say that it was the same ocean of universal consciousness, and even if not stated in so many words, he had
dared to imply that this consciousness proclaimed all men
one; all nations and races met in the universal world of the
dream; and he had dared to say that the dream-symbol could
be interpreted; its language, its imagery were common to the
whole race, not only of the living but of those ten thousand
years dead. The picture-writing, the hieroglyph of the dream,
was the common property of the whole race; in the dream,
man, as at the beginning of time, spoke a universal language,
and man, meeting in the universal understanding of the
unconscious or the subconscious, would forgo barriers of time
and space, and man, understanding man, would save
mankind.

54

WITH PRECISE Jewish instinct for the particular in the general,
for the personal in the impersonal or universal, for the *material*
in the abstract, he had dared to plunge into the unexplored

depth, first of his own unconscious or subconscious being. From it, he dredged, as samples of his theories, his own dreams, exposing them as serious discoveries, facts, with cause and effect, beginning and end, often showing from even the most trivial dream sequence the powerful dramatic impact that projected it. He took the events of the day preceding the night of the dream, the dream-day as he called it; he unravelled from the mixed conditions and contacts of the ordinary affairs of life the particular thread that went on spinning its length through the substance of the mind, the *buried* mind, the sleeping, the unconscious or subconscious mind. The thread so eagerly identified as part of the pattern, part of some commonplace or some intricate or intimate matter of the waking life, would as likely as not be lost, at the precise moment when, identified, it showed its shimmering or its drab dream-substance. The sleeping mind was not one, not all equally sleeping; part of the unconscious mind would become conscious at a least expected moment; this part of the dreaming mind that laid traps or tricked the watcher or slammed doors on the scene or the unravelling tapestry of the dream sequence he called the Censor; it was guardian at the gates of the underworld, like the dog Cerberus, of Hell.

55

IN THE DREAM MATTER were Heaven and Hell, and he spared himself and his first avidly curious, mildly shocked readers neither. He did not spare himself or his later growing public, but others he spared. He would break off a most interesting dream-narrative, to explain that personal matter, concerning *not himself,* had intruded. *Know thyself,* said the ironic Delphic oracle, and the sage or priest who framed the utterance knew that to know yourself in the full sense of the words was to know everybody. *Know thyself,* said the Professor, and plunging time and again, he amassed that store of intimate revelation contained in his impressive volumes. But to *know thyself,* to set forth the knowledge, brought down not only a storm of abuse from high-placed doctors, psychologists, scientists, and other accredited intellectuals the world over, but made his very name almost a by-word for illiterate quips, unseemly jokes, and general ridicule.

56

MAYBE HE LAUGHED at the jokes, I don't know. His beautiful mouth seemed always slightly smiling, though his eyes, set deep and slightly asymmetrical under the domed forehead (with those furrows cut by a master chisel), were unrevealing. His eyes did not speak to me. I cannot even say that they were sad eyes. If at a moment of distress – as when I went to him that day when all the doors in Vienna were closed and the streets empty – there came that pause that sometimes fell between us, he, sensing some almost unbearable anxiety and tension in me, would break this spell with some kindly old-world courtesy, some question: What had I been reading? Did I find the books I wanted in the library his wife's sister had recommended? Of course – if I wanted any of his books at any time – Had I heard again from Bryher, from my daughter? Had I heard lately from America?

I would have taken the hour-glass in my hand and set it the other way round so that the sands of his life would have as many years to run forward as now ran backward. Or I would have slipped through a secret door – only I would have the right to do this – and entreat a kindly Being. (Only I could do this, for my gift must be something different.) I would change my years for his; it would not be as generous a number as I could have wished for him, yet it would make a difference. Perhaps there would be twenty years, even thirty years left in my hour-glass. 'Look,' I would say to this kindly Being, 'those two on your shelf there – just make the slightest alteration of the hour-glasses. Put H.D. in the place of Sigmund Freud (I will still have a few years left in which to tidy up my not very important affairs). It's not too much to ask of you. And it can be done. Someone did it or offered to do it in a play once. It was a Greek play, wasn't it? A woman – I don't remember her name – offered her years in exchange – to someone else – for something. What was it? There was Hercules or Herakles and a struggle with Death. Was the play called *Alcestis?* I wonder. And of course, one of those three must have written – there they are on the top of the Professor's case, to the right of the wide-opened double door that leads into his inner sanctum. Aeschylus? Sophocles? Euripides? Who wrote the *Alcestis?* But it doesn't really matter who wrote it, for the play is going on now – at any rate we are acting it, the old Professor and I. The old Professor doubles the part. He is Hercules struggling with Death and he is the beloved, about to die. Moreover he himself, in his own character, has made the dead live, has summoned a host of dead and dying children from the living tomb.'

57

WHEN I SAID TO HIM one day that time went too quickly (did he or didn't he feel that?) he struck a semi-comic attitude, he threw his arm forward as if ironically addressing an invisible presence or an imaginary audience. *'Time,'* he said. The word was uttered in his inimitable, two-edged manner; he seemed to defy the creature, the abstraction; into that one word, he seemed to pack a store of contradictory emotions; there was irony, entreaty, defiance, with a vague, tender pathos. It seemed as if the word was surcharged, an explosive that might, at any minute, go off. (Many of his words did, in a sense, explode, blasting down prisons, useless dykes and dams, bringing down landslides, it is true, but opening up mines of hidden treasure.) *'Time,'* he said again, more quietly, and then, *'time gallops.'*

'Time gallops withal.' I wonder if he knew that he was quoting Shakespeare? Though the exact application of Rosalind's elaborate quip about Time hardly seems appropriate. 'Who doth he gallop withal?' asks Orlando. And Rosalind answers, 'With a thief to the gallows; for though he go as softly as foot can fall, he thinks himself too soon there.' But a thief certainly; in a greater dramatic tradition, he had stolen fire, like Prometheus, from heaven.

58

STOP THIEF! But nothing could stop him, once he started unearthing buried treasures (he called it striking oil). And anyhow, wasn't it his own? Hadn't he found it? But *stop thief,* they shouted or worse. He was nonchalantly unlocking vaults and caves, taking down the barriers that generations had carefully set up against their hidden motives, their secret ambitions, their suppressed desires. *Stop thief!* Admit, however, that what he offered as treasure, this revelation that he seemed to value, was poor stuff, trash indeed, ideas that a ragpicker would pass over in disdain, old junk stored in the attic, put away, forgotten, not even worth the trouble of cutting up for firewood, cumbersome at that, difficult to move, and moreover if you started to move one unwieldly cumbersome idea, you might dislodge the whole cart-load of junk; it had been there such a long time, it was almost part of the wall and the attic ceiling of the house of life. *Stop thief!* But why, after all, stop him? His so-called discoveries were patently ridiculous. Time gallops withal ... with a thief to the gallows. And give a man enough rope – we have heard somewhere – and he will hang himself!

59

HE WAS A LITTLE SURPRISED at the outburst. He had not thought that detached and lofty practitioners and men of science could be so angry at what was, after all, chapter and verse, a contribution to a branch of abstract thought, applied to medical science. He had worked with the famous Dr. Charcot in Paris. There are other names that figure in the historical account given us by Professor Freud himself in his short *Autobiographical Study*. We have the names of doctors, famous specialists, who gave an idea to Freud; we have Freud himself impartially dividing honors between Breuer (or whoever it happens to be) and Freud. We have Freud himself giving Freud credit for the discovery of the cocaine anesthesia attributed to Koller. But when I asked the analyst Walter Schmideberg when and how the Professor happened on the idea that led to his linking up neurotic states of megalomania and aggrandizement with, in certain instances, fantasies of youth and childhood, he answered me correctly and conventionally; he said that Freud did not happen on ideas. I wonder? And said I wondered. But Mr. Schmideberg repeated what already, of course, I was supposed to know, that the whole established body of work was founded on accurate and accumulated data of scientific observation. That is not what I asked. I wanted to know at what exact moment, and in what manner, there came that flash of inspiration, that thing that clicked, that sounded, that shouted in the inner Freud mind, heart, or soul, *this is it.*

But things don't happen like that. Or do they? At least we are free to wonder. We ourselves are free to imagine, to reconstruct, to *see* even, as in a play or film, those characters, in their precise setting, the Paris of that period, 1885. Dr. Charcot was concerned with hysteria and neurotics this side of the border-line. That border-line, it is true, was of necessity but vaguely indicated; there were hysterics, neurotics on this side and the actual insane on the other but there was a wide gap for all that, an unexplored waste-land, a no-man's-land between them. At least there was a no-man's-land; at least there were cases that not so very long ago would have been isolated as insane that now came under a milder rule, the kingdom of hysteria. The world of medical knowledge had made vast strides for there was still a memory in the minds of the older generations of eye-witness tales of a time, here in this very city, when the inmates of the insane asylums were fastened with chains, like wild beasts, to the walls or to iron rails or stakes; moreover, the public was admitted at stated intervals to view the wild animals in the course of a holiday tour of the city. That time was past, not so very long past, it is true, yet past, due to the humanitarian efforts of the preceding generation of scientists and doctors. They had progressed certainly. And our Professor could, in point of fact, have visited the more 'modern' foundations of that time and place. Paris? He was a stranger. 1870 was by no means forgotten. He had seen the fangs of the pack during his student days. He writes of his early days at the University in Vienna, 'Above all, I found that I was expected to feel myself inferior and alien because I was a Jew.' He adds, 'I refused absolutely to do the first of these things.' But there were others, here in Paris, inferiors, aliens certainly, who dwelt apart from their fellow men, not chained, though still (in more human surroundings) segregated, separated, in little rooms, we may conclude, or cells with bars before the windows or doors. An improvement certainly. They too 'refused absolutely' to feel themselves inferior. On the contrary. These were special cases, but there was the great crowd at large, under observation at the Salpêtrière. But among the hysterical cases under Charcot's observation and the insane of the young Freud's own private consideration, there were incidents, unnoted or minimized by the various doctors and observers, which yet held matter worth grave consideration. He noted how the disconnected sequence of the apparently unrelated actions of certain of the patients yet suggested a sort of order, followed a pattern like the broken sequence of events in a half-remembered dream. Dream? Was the dream then, in its turn, projected or suggested by events in the daily life, was the dream the counter-coin side of madness or was madness a waking dream? There was an odd element of tragedy sometimes, something not always wholly on the physical or sordid material level. It was Hell, of course. But these people in Hell sometimes bore strange resemblance to things he had remembered, things he had read about, old kings in old countries, women broken by wars, and enslaved, distorted children.

There were bars before some of the cells (in this scene built up purely from our own intuitive imagination), yet these cages sometimes presented scenes as from a play. Caesar strutted there. There Hannibal – Hannibal? Why Hannibal? As a boy he himself had worshipped Hannibal, imagined himself in the rôle of world-conqueror. But every boy at some time or another strutted with imaginary sword and armor. *Every boy?* This man, this Caesar, who flung his toga over his arm with a not altogether unauthentic gesture, might simply be living out some childish fantasy. If he could examine the patient in suitable surroundings – but the patient shouted *et tu Brute* and became violent at any suggestion of approach or friendly contact. If he could have interviewed this Caesar a few years back – he had been a man of some prominence at one time – he might have been able to worm out of him the secret of his Caesar mania. The mind was clouded now but there was no report in this case of actual tissue decay or the usual physical symptoms that end inevitably in madness. Caesar? Hannibal? These were outstanding recognizable historical personages. But were these the entities that caused this – *fixation* was a word not yet coined in this connection. This man was acting a part, Caesar. Caesar? He himself, as a child, enacted a similar rôle, Hannibal. But was it Hannibal? Was it Caesar? Was it – ? Well, yes – it might be – how odd. Yes – it could be! It might be this man's father now that he was impersonating – wasn't the father the Caesar, the conqueror, the symbol of power, the Czar, Kaiser, the King in the child's kingdom – admittedly small but to the child of vast worldwide importance, the world to him, his home. The whole world for a child is its home, its father, mother, brothers, sisters, and so on – its school later and friends from other 'kingdoms.' Why, yes – how clear it all was – this Caesar now? How had it come about? There must be something behind this collapse not noted in the record of the patient's physical and even mental conditions and symptoms. There must be something else behind many of the cases here and at the Salpêtrière – not all of them – but some of them – and other cases. . . . There must be something behind the whole build-up of present-day medical science – there must be something further on or deeper down – there must be something that would reveal the secrets of these states of glorified personality and other states and conditions – there must be something. . . . Why, Hannibal! There is Caesar behind bars – here is Hannibal, here am I, Sigmund Freud, watching Caesar behind bars. But it was Caesar who was conqueror – was he? – I came, I saw, I conquered – yes, I will conquer. I will. I, Hannibal – not Caesar. I, the despised Carthaginian, I, the enemy of Rome. I, Hannibal. So you see, I, Sigmund Freud, myself standing here, a favorite and gifted, admit it, student of Dr. Charcot, in no way to all appearances deranged or essentially peculiar, true to my own orbit – *true to my own orbit?* True to my own orbit, my childhood fantasies of Hannibal, my identification with Hannibal, the Carthaginian (Jew, not Roman) – I, Sigmund Freud, understand this Caesar. I, Hannibal!

And Caesar's wife too (if we may continue our build-up of this purely imaginative sequence of cause and effect), there is Caesar's wife to be considered. This particular lady was not even an out-patient of this particular institution, but she might soon be. She was found lingering in the waiting room, after the others had left. She was always demanding interviews with the doctors and the superintendent himself, getting in everyone's way. It was becoming quite a feature with the institution, the superintendent had left special orders that he was not to be disturbed, he had been compelled to deny her the last private interview she demanded; the famous specialist was overworked, there was too much to be done here, everywhere, trying personal entanglements must be avoided at all costs. *Personal entanglements?* But this good lady would be the first to decry any such shadow of design on her part. But wasn't that her trouble? She had been devoted to her husband, the separation was affecting her, she herself seemed on the verge of a serious breakdown. That was only natural, wasn't it, under the tragic circumstances? But this sort of suppressed neurotic symptom – *symptom?* This sort of separation between two people long married and devoted might have serious repercussions, actually throw the whole nervous system out of gear, unbalance the delicately adjusted mechanism of the mind itself. Her worry had worn on her – poor woman – and no wonder. Someone should look after her. But she was not even an out-patient, it wasn't their business to probe into the personal affairs of the patients' wives and families. *Affairs?* Caesar's wife? Yes, she was Caesar's wife, obviously above suspicion, a conventional woman yet a woman of the world. Such things had happened before. Where was his thought taking him? There had been other cases here – that girl whose happiness at the news of her husband's possible return from Algiers after a long absence had so improved her condition that Dr. Charcot, consulted in this instance, had himself suggested her leaving the hospital for a time. Her health, it was reported, had improved after her return to her husband, but *if her husband went away again would her symptoms return?*

60

THIS OBVIOUSLY IS NOT an historical account of the preliminary steps that led to the establishment of a new branch of psychological research and a new form of healing called psychoanalysis. The actual facts are accessible to any serious student of Professor Freud's work. But it seems to me it might have been through some such process of inner reasoning that the theme opened. The *theme?* I write the word and wonder why I write it. It seemed to me to suggest music – yes, musical terms do seem relevant to the curious and original process of the Professor's intuitive reasoning that led up to, developed, amplified, simplified the first astonishing findings of the young Viennese doctor whom the diagnoses of his elders and betters had not always satisfied. It was not only that the young Sigmund Freud was astute, methodical, conscientious, subtle, clever, original – though he was all these. It was not only that he came from a race that had venerated learning and (like the Arabs) had preserved, in spite of repeated persecutions, a singular *feeling* for medicine, along with mathematics and certain forms of abstract philosophy and poetry, at a time when (as now) the liberal and applied arts seemed overshadowed with the black wing of man's growing power of destruction and threat of racial separateness. He stood alone and we may imagine that he was singularly proud, though of so genial a nature, so courteous a manner, and so delicate a wit; he was easy to get on with, he could discourse delightfully on any subject, at any time, with anybody. But what was it about him? His appearance, his habits, his way of life were conventional enough; even his worst enemies could find nothing to criticize about his private life; he was strictly correct, almost orthodox, you might say.

The point was that for all his amazing originality, he was drawing from a source so deep in human consciousness that the outer rock or shale, the accumulation of hundreds or thousands of years of casual, slack, or even wrong or evil thinking, had all but sealed up the original spring or well-head. He called it striking oil, but others – long ago – had dipped into that same spring. They called it 'a well of living water' in the old days, or simply the 'still waters.' The Professor spoke of this source of inspiration in terms of oil. It focused the abstraction, made it concrete, a modern business symbol. Although it was obvious that he was speaking of a vague, vast abstraction, he used a common, almost a commonplace, symbol for it. He used the idiom or slang of the counting-house, of Wall Street, a businessman's concrete definite image for a successful run of luck or hope of success in the if-we-should-strike-oil or old-so-and-so-has-struck-oil-again manner. 'I struck oil but there is enough left for fifty, for one hundred years or more.' It is diffi·cult to imagine the Professor saying solemnly, 'I drew by right of inheritance from the great source of inspiration of Israel and the Psalmist – Jeremiah, some might call me. I stumbled on a well of living water, the river of life. It ran muddy or bright. It was blocked by fallen logs, some petrified – and an accumulation of decaying leaves and branches. I saw the course of the river and how it ran, and I, personally, cleared away a bit of rubbish, so that at least a small section of the river should run clear. There is a lot yet to be done – for a hundred years or more – so that all men, all nations, may gather together, understanding in the end. . . .' But no, that was not the Professor's way of talking. 'I struck oil' suggests business enterprise. We visualize stark uprights and skeleton-like steel cages, like unfinished Eiffel Towers. And there are many, I have reason to know, who think of the whole method or system of psychoanalysis in some such terms, a cage, some mechanical construction set up in an arid desert, to trap the unwary, and if there is 'oil' to be inferred, the 'oil' goes to someone else; there are astute doctors who 'squeeze you dry' with their exorbitant fees for prolonged and expensive treatments. A tiresome subject at best – have nothing to do with it – it's worn out, dated; true, it was fashionable enough among the young intellectuals after the First World War but they turned out a dreary lot and who, after all, has heard of any of them since?

61

TIRESOME INDEED! So is Aeschylus tiresome to most people, so is Sophocles, so is Plato and that old Socrates with his tedious matter and his more than tedious manner. The Socratic method? That was a business of egging on an intellectual contestant, almost in the manner of a fencer with pin-pricks – wasn't it? – or sword-pricks of prodding questions that would eventually bring the debatable matter to a head, so that the fight could be open and above-board, unless the rival were slain in the preliminary clash of intellectual steel. There was something of that in the Professor's method of analytic treatment, but there was a marked difference. The question must be propounded by the protagonist himself, he must dig it out from its buried hiding-place, he himself must find the question before it could be answered.

62

HE HIMSELF must clear away his own rubbish, before his particular stream, his personal life, could run clear of obstruction into the great river of humanity, hence to the sea of superhuman perfection, the 'Absolute,' as Socrates or Plato called it.

63

BUT WE ARE here today in a city of ruin, a world ruined, it might seem, almost past redemption. We must forgo a flight from reality into the green pastures or the cool recesses of the

Academe; though those pastures and those gardens have out-
lasted many ruined cities and threat of world ruin; we are not
ready for discussion of the Absolute, Absolute Beauty, Absolute Truth, Absolute Goodness. We have rested in the pastures, we have wandered beside those still waters, we have
sensed the fragrance of the myrtle thickets beyond distant
hedges, and the groves of flowering citrons. *Kennst du das Land?*
Oh yes, Professor, I know it very well. But I am remembering
the injunction you laid upon me and I am thinking of my fel-
low-pupil whose place you say I have taken, my brother-in-
arms, the Flying Dutchman, who, intellectually gifted
beyond the ordinary run of man, endowed with Eastern
islands and plantations, trained to a Western discipline of
mind and body, yet flew too high and flew too quickly.

64

THE PROFESSOR is speaking to me very seriously. This is in his
study in Vienna a few weeks after I had first begun my work
there. 'I am asking only one thing of you,' he said. Even as I
write the words, I have the same sense of anxiety, of tension, of
imminent responsibility that I had at that moment. What can
he possibly be going to say? What can he ask me to do? Or not
to do? More likely a *shalt not* than a demand for some specific
act or course of action. His manner was serious yet kindly. Yet
in spite of that or because of that, I felt like a child, summoned
to my father's study or my mother's sewing room or told by a
teacher to wait in after school, after the others had left, for
those 'few words' that were for myself alone. *Stop thief!* What
had I done? What was I likely to do? 'I ask only one thing of
you children' – my mother's very words.

65

FOR THE PROFESSOR is standing in his study. The Professor is asking only one thing of me. I was right in my premonition, it is a *shalt not*. He is asking something of me, confiding in me, treating me in his courteous, subtle way as an intellectual equal. He is very firm about this, however, and he is patiently explaining it to me. 'Of course, you understand' is the offhand way in which he offers me, from time to time, some rare discovery, some priceless finding, or 'Perhaps you may feel differently,' as if my feelings, my discoveries, were on a par with his own. He does not lay down the law, only this once – this one law. He says, 'Please, never – I mean, never at any time, in any circumstance, endeavor to defend me, if and when you hear abusive remarks made about me and my work.'

He explained it carefully. He might have been giving a lesson in geometry or demonstrating the inevitable course of a disease once the virus has entered the system. At this point, he seemed to indicate (as if there were a chart of a fever patient, pinned on the wall before us), at the least suggestion that you may be about to begin a counter-argument in my defense, the anger or the frustration of the assailant will be driven deeper. You will do no good to the detractor by mistakenly beginning a logical defense. You will drive the hatred or the fear or the prejudice in deeper. You will do no good to yourself, for you will only expose your own feelings – I take for granted that you have deep feelings about my discoveries, or you would not be here. You will do no good to me and my work, for antagonism, once taking hold, cannot be rooted out from above the surface, and it thrives, in a way, on heated argument and digs in deeper. The only way to extract the fear or prejudice would be from within, from below, and as naturally this type of prejudiced or frightened mind would dodge any hint of a suggestion of psychoanalytic treatment or even, put it, study and research along these lines, you cannot get at the root of the trouble. Every word, spoken in my defense, I mean, to already prejudiced individuals, serves to drive the root in deeper. If the matter is ignored, the attacker may forgo his anger – or in time, even, his unconscious mind may find another object on which to fix its tentacles. . . .

This was the gist of the matter. In our talks together he rarely used any of the now rather overworked technical terms, invented by himself and elaborated on by the growing body of doctors, psychologists, and nerve specialists who form the somewhat formidable body of the International Psycho-Analytical Association. When, on one occasion, I was endeavoring to explain a matter in which my mind tugged two ways, I said, 'I suppose you would say it was a matter of ambivalence?' And as he did not answer me, I said, 'Or do you say am-*bi*-valence? I don't know whether it's pronounced ambi-*valence* or am-*bi*-valence.' The Professor's arm shot forward as it did on those occasions when he wished to stress a finding or focus my attention to some point in hand; he said, in his curiously casual ironical manner, 'Do you know, I myself have always wondered. I often wish that I could find someone to explain these matters to me.'

66

THERE WAS SO MUCH to be explained, so little time in which to do it. My serpent-and-thistle motive, for instance, or *Leitmotiv*, I had almost written. It was a sign, a symbol certainly – it must have been – but even if I had found another seal-ring like the one I saw in Paris, among that handful of old rings in the corner of the shelf in the other room, it wouldn't have proved anything and might have led us too far afield in a discussion or reconstruction of cause and effect, which might indeed have included priceless treasures, gems, and jewels, among the so-called findings of the unconscious mind revealed by the dream-content or associated thought and memory, yet have side-tracked the issue in hand. My serpent and thistle – what did it remind me of? There was Aaron's rod, of course, which when flung to the ground turned into a living reptile. Reptile? Aaron's rod, if I am not mistaken, was originally the staff of Moses. There was Moses in the bulrushes, 'our' dream and 'our' Princess. There was the ground, cursed by God because Adam and Eve had eaten of the Fruit of the Tree. Henceforth, it would bring forth thorns and thistles – thorns, thistles, the words conjure up the same scene, the barren, unproductive waste or desert. *Do men gather grapes of thorns, or figs of thistles?* Another question, another question mark, a half-*S*, the other way round, *S* for *s*eal, *s*ymbol, *s*erpent certainly, *s*ignet, *S*igmund.

67

Sigmund, the singing voice; no, it is Siegmund really, the victorious mouth or voice or utterance. There was Victory, our sign on the wall, our hieroglyph, our writing. There was the tiny bronze, his favorite among the semicircle of the Gods or as 'other people read: Goods' on his table. There was Niké, Victory, and Niké A-pteros, the Wingless Victory, for Victory could never, would never fly away from Athens. There was

Athens, a city set on a hill; hill, mountain; there was Berg-gasse, the hill, *Berg,* and the path or street or way, *gasse.* There were designs, weren't there, of acanthus leaves to crown upright Corinthian capitals? And the Latin *acanthus,* and the related Greek word *akantha,* is thorn or prickle. There were patterns, decorative hieroglyphs of acanthus leaves, a very classic symbol; and there was a crown, we have been told, in the end, of thorns.

68

BUT TO OUR LITTLE abridged Greek Lexicon, to verify *akantha.* Yes – as from *aké,* a point, edge, hence a prickly plant, thistle; also a thorny tree. *A thorny tree.* Was our thistle the sign or sigil of all thorny trees? Perhaps even of that singularly prickly Tree of the Knowledge of Good and Evil with its attendant Serpent. There were, and are, many varieties of serpents. There was, among many others, that serpent of Wisdom that crouched at the feet of the goddess Athené and was one of her attributes, like the spear (*aké,* a point) she held in her hand – though we cannot be sure that it was a spear that the Professor's perfect little bronze once held in her hand. It might have been a rod or staff.

69

THY ROD AND THY STAFF. In England, our American gold-enrod, that runs riot in the late-summer fields and along every lane and at the edge of every strip of woodland, is cultivated in tidy clumps in gardens, and is called Aaron's rod. The gold-enrod brings us to the Golden Bough; it was to Plato that Meleager, in the Greek Anthology, attributed the golden bough, ever shining with its own light. And the Professor, one winter day, offered me a little branch. He explained that his son in the South of France had posted (or sent by some acquaintance returning to Vienna from the Midi) a box of oranges, and some branches with leaves were among them. He thought I might like this. I took the branch, a tiny tree in itself, with its cluster of golden fruit. I thanked the Professor. At least, I murmured some platitude, 'How lovely – how charming of you' or some such. Did he know, did he ever know, or did he ever not-know, what I was thinking? I did not say what I had no time to formulate into words – or if I had had time for other than a superficial 'How lovely – how perfectly charming,' I could not have trusted myself to say the words. They were there. They were singing. They went on singing like an echo of an echo in a shell – very far away yet very near – the very shell substance of my outer ear and the curled involuted or convoluted shell skull, and inside the skull, the curled, intricate, hermit-like mollusk, the brain-matter itself. Thoughts are things – sometimes they are songs. I did not have to recall the words, I had not written them. Another mollusk in a hard cap of bone or shell had projected these words. There was a song set to them, that still another singing skull had fashioned. No, not Schumann's music – lovely as it is – there was a song we sang as school-children, another setting to the words. And even the words sing themselves without music, so it does not matter that I have not been able to identify the 'tune' as we lilted it. *Kennst du das Land?*

70

Kennst du das Land, wo die Zitronen blühn?

THE WORDS RETURN with singular freshness and poignancy, as I, after this long time of waiting, am able to remember without unbearable terror and overwhelming heartbreak those sessions in Vienna. The war closed on us, before I had time to sort out, relive, and reassemble the singular series of events and dreams that belonged in historical time to the 1914–1919 period. I wanted to dig down and dig out, root out my personal weeds, strengthen my purpose, reaffirm my beliefs, canalize my energies, and I seized on the unexpected chance of working with Professor Freud himself. I could never have thought it possible to approach him, nor even have thought of inquiring if it were possible, if it had not been for Dr. Sachs's suggestion. I had had some fascinating, preliminary talks with Dr. Hanns Sachs in Berlin and wanted to go on with the work, but he was leaving for America. Dr. Sachs asked me if I would consider working with the Professor if he would take me? If he would take me? It seemed such a fantastic suggestion and to my mind highly unlikely that Freud himself would consider me as analysand or student. But *if* the Professor would accept me, I would have no choice whatever in the matter. I would go to him, of course.

71

I HAVE SAID earlier in these notes that the Professor's explanations were too illuminating or too depressing. I meant that in some strange way we had managed to get at the root of things, *today, we have tunneled very deep;* and in another still stranger way, we had approached the clearest fountain-head of highest truth, as in the luminous *real* dream of the Princess and the river which was in the realm of what is known generally as the supernormal; it was a scene or picture from those realms from which the *illuminati* received their – 'credentials' seems a strange word as I write it, but it 'wrote itself.' My Princess picture was one of an exquisite, endless sequence from an *illuminated manuscript,* and has its place in that category among books and manuscripts; the dream, you may remember, I said in the beginning, varies like the people we meet, like the books we read. The books and the people merge in this world of fantasy and imagination; nonetheless we may differentiate with the utmost felicity and fidelity between dreams and the types of different fantasies; there are the most trivial and tiresome dreams, the newspaper class – but even there is, in an old newspaper, sometimes a hint of eternal truth, or a quotation from a great man's speech or some tale of heroism, among the trashy and often sordid and trivial record of the day's events. The printed page varies, cheap news-print, good print, bad print, smudged and uneven print – there are the great letter words of an advertisement or the almost invisible pin-print; there are the huge capitals of a child's alphabet chart or building blocks; letters or ideas may run askew on the page, as it were; they may be purposeless; they may be stereotyped and not meant for 'reading' but as a test, as for example the symmetrical letters that don't of necessity 'spell' anything, on a doctor's or oculist's chart hung on the wall in an office or above a bed in a hospital. There are dreams or sequences of dreams that follow a line like a graph on a map or show a jagged triangular pattern, like a crack on a bowl that shows the bowl or vase may at any moment fall in pieces; we all know

that almost invisible thread-line on the cherished glass but-
ter-dish that predicts it will 'come apart in me 'ands' sooner or
later – sooner, more likely.

There are all these shapes, lines, graphs, the *hieroglyph of the
unconscious,* and the Professor had first opened the field to the
study of this vast, unexplored region. He himself – at least to
me personally – deplored the tendency to *fix* ideas too firmly to
set symbols, or to weld them inexorably. It is true that he himself started to decipher or decode the vast accumulation of the
material of the unconscious mind; it was he who 'struck oil'
but the application of the 'oil,' what could or should be made
of it, could not be entirely regulated or supervised by its original 'promoter.' He struck oil; certainly there was 'something
in it'; yes, a vast field for exploration and – alas – exploitation
lay open. There were the immemorial Gods ranged in their
semicircle on the Professor's table, that stood, as I have said,
like the high altar in the Holy of Holies. There were those
Gods, each the carved symbol of an idea or a deathless dream,
that some people read: Goods.

72

THERE ARE THE WISE and the foolish virgins and their several
lamps. *Thou anointest my head with oil* – the oil of understanding
– and, indeed, *my cup runneth over.* But this purposes to be a personal reconstruction of intention and impression. I had begun
my preliminary research in order to fortify and equip myself
to face war when it came, and to help in some subsidiary way,
if my training were sufficient and my aptitudes suitable, with
war-shocked and war-shattered people. But my actual personal war-shock (1914–1919) did not have a chance. My sessions with the Professor were barely under way, before there

were preliminary signs and symbols of the approaching ordeal. And the thing I primarily wanted to fight in the open, war, its cause and effect, with its inevitable aftermath of neurotic breakdown and related nerve disorders, was driven deeper. With the death-head swastika chalked on the pavement, leading to the Professor's very door, I must, in all decency, calm as best I could my own personal Phobia, my own personal little Dragon of war-terror, and with whatever power I could summon or command order him off, for the time being at any rate, back to his subterranean cavern.

There he growled and bit on his chains and was only loosed finally, when the full apocryphal terror of fire and brimstone, of whirlwind and flood and tempest, of the Biblical Day of Judgment and the Last Trump, became no longer abstractions, terrors too dreadful to be thought of, but things that were happening every day, every night, and at one time, at every hour of the day and night, to myself and my friends, and all the wonderful and all the drab and ordinary London people.

73

AND THE KINDLY Being whom I would have entreated had wafted the old Professor out of it. He had gone before the blast and bombing and fires had devastated this city; he was a handful of ashes, cherished in an urn or scattered among the grass and flowers in one of the Gardens of Remembrance, outside London. I suppose there must be a marble slab there on the garden wall or a little box in a niche beside a garden path. I have not even gone to look, to regard a familiar name with a date perhaps, and wander along a path, hedged with clipped yew or, more likely, fragrant dust-green lavender, and think of the Professor. For our Garden of Remembrance is somewhere else.

Kennst du das Land, wo die Zitronen blühn,
Im dunkeln Laub die Gold-Orangen glühn,
Ein sanfter Wind vom blauen Himmel weht,
Die Myrte still und hoch der Lorbeer steht,
Kennst du es wohl?
Dahin! Dahin
Möcht ich mit dir, o mein Geliebter, ziehn.

Kennst du das Haus? Auf Säulen ruht sein
Dach,
Es glänzt der Saal, es schimmert das Gemach,
Und Marmorbilder stehn und sehn mich an:
Was hat man dir, du armes Kind, getan?
Kennst du es wohl?
Dahin! Dahin
Möcht ich mit dir, o mein Beschützer, ziehn.

Kennst du den Berg und seinen Wolkensteg?
Das Maultier sucht im Nebel seinen Weg,
In Höhlen wohnt der Drachen alte Brut,
Es stürzt der Fels und über ihn die Flut;
Kennst du ihn wohl?
Dahin! Dahin
Geht unser Weg! o Vater, lass uns ziehn!

74

I HAVE SAID that these impressions must take me, rather than I take them. The first impression of all takes me back to the beginning, to my first session with the Professor. Paula has opened the door (though I did not then know that the pretty little Viennese maid was called Paula). She has divested me of my coat and made some welcoming remark which has slightly embarrassed me, as I am thinking English thoughts and only English words come to prompt me. She has shown me into the waiting room with the lace curtains at the window, with framed photographs of celebrities, some known personally to me; Dr. Havelock Ellis and Dr. Hanns Sachs gaze at me, familiar but a little distorted in their frames under the reflecting glass. There is the modest, treasured, framed diploma from the small New England university, which I examined later, and the macabre, detailed, Düreresque symbolic drawing, a 'Buried Alive' or of some such school of thought. I wait in this room. I know that Prof. Dr. Sigmund Freud will open the door which faces me. Although I know this and have been preparing for some months for this ordeal, I am, nonetheless, taken aback, surprised, shocked even, when the door opens. It seems to me, after my time of waiting, that he appears too suddenly.

Automatically, I walk through the door. It closes. Sigmund Freud does not speak. He is waiting for me to say something. I cannot speak. I look around the room. A lover of Greek art, I am automatically taking stock of the room's contents. Pricelessly lovely objects are displayed here on the shelves to right, to left of me. I have been told about the Professor, his family, his way of life. I have heard certain personal anecdotes not available to the general readers of his books. I have heard him lovingly criticized by his adorers and soundly berated by his enemies. I know that he had a very grave recurrence of a former serious illness, some five years or so ago, and was again operated on for that particularly pernicious form of cancer of the mouth or tongue, and that by a miracle (to the amazement of the Viennese specialists) he recovered. It seems to me, in some curious way, that we were both 'miraculously saved' for some purpose. But all this is a feeling, an atmosphere – something that I realize or perceive, but do not actually put into words or thoughts. I could not have said this even if I had, at that moment, realized it. I do know that it is a great privilege to be here, this I do actually realize. I am here because Dr. Sachs suggested my coming here and wrote the Professor about me. Dr. Sachs had talked lovingly about the Professor and, sometimes in gentle irony, had spoken of the 'poor Frau Professor.' But no one had told me that this room was lined with treasures. I was to greet the Old Man of the Sea, but no one had told me of the treasures he had salvaged from the sea-depth.

75

HE IS AT home here. He is part and parcel of these treasures. I have come a long way, I have brought nothing with me. He has his family, the tradition of an unbroken family, reaching back through this old heart of the Roman Empire, further into the Holy Land.

> *Ah, Psyche, from the regions which*
> *Are Holy Land!*

He is the infinitely old symbol, weighing the soul, Psyche, in the Balance. Does the Soul, passing the portals of life, entering the House of Eternity, greet the Keeper of the Door? It seems so. I should have thought the Door-Keeper, at home beyond the threshold, might have greeted the shivering soul. Not so, the Professor. But waiting and finding that I would not or could not speak, he uttered. What he said – and I thought a little sadly – was, 'You are the only person who has ever come into this room and looked at the things in the room before looking at me.'

But worse was to come. A little lion-like creature came padding toward me – a lioness, as it happened. She had emerged from the inner sanctum or manifested from under or behind the couch; anyhow, she continued her course across the carpet. Embarrassed, shy, overwhelmed, I bend down to greet this creature. But the Professor says, 'Do not touch her – she snaps – she is very difficult with strangers.' *Strangers?* Is the Soul crossing the threshold a stranger to the Door-Keeper? It appears so. But, though no accredited dog-lover, I like dogs and they oddly and sometimes unexpectedly 'take' to me. If this is an exception, I am ready to take the risk. Unintimidated but distressed by the Professor's somewhat forbidding manner, I not only continue my gesture toward the little chow, but crouch on the floor so that she can snap better if she wants to. Yofi – her name is Yofi – snuggles her nose into my hand and nuzzles her head, in delicate sympathy, against my shoulder.

76

So AGAIN I can say the Professor was not always right. That is, yes, he was always right in his judgments, but my form of rightness, my intuition, sometimes functioned by the split-second (that makes all the difference in spiritual time-computations) the quicker. I was swifter in some intuitive instances, and sometimes a small tendril of a root from that great common Tree of Knowledge went deeper into the sub-soil. His were the great giant roots of that tree, but mine, with hair-like almost invisible feelers, sometimes quivered a warning or resolved a problem, as for instance at the impact of that word *stranger*. 'We'll show him,' retorts the invisible intuitive root-let; and, without forming the thought, the words 'love me, love my dog' are there to prompt me. 'He will see whether or not I am indifferent,' my *emotion* snaps back, though not in words. 'If he is so wise, so clever,' the smallest possible sub-soil rootlet gives its message, 'you show him that you too are wise, are clever. Show him that you have ways of finding out things about people, other than looking at their mere outward ordinary appearance.' My intuition challenges the Professor, though not in words. That intuition cannot really be translated into words, but if it could be it would go, roughly, something like this: 'Why should I look at you? You are contained in the things you love, and if you accuse me of looking at the things in the room before looking at you, well, I will go on looking at the things in the room. One of them is this little golden dog. She snaps, does she? You call me a stranger, do you? Well, I will show you two things: one, I am not a stranger; two, even if I were, two seconds ago, I am now no longer one. And moreover I never was a stranger to this little golden Yofi.'

The wordless challenge goes on, 'You are a very great man. I am overwhelmed with embarrassment, I am shy and frightened and gauche as an over-grown school-girl. But listen. You are a man. Yofi is a dog. I am a woman. If this dog and this woman "take" to one another, it will prove that beyond your caustic implied criticism – if criticism it is – there is another region of cause and effect, another region of question and answer.' Undoubtedly, the Professor took an important clue from the first reaction of a new analysand or patient. I was, as it happened, not prepared for this. It would have been worse for me if I had been.

77

'BY CHANCE OR intention,' I started these notes on September 19th. Consulting my 'Mysteries of the Ancients' calendar, I find Dr. W. B. Crow has assigned this date to 'Thoth, Egyptian form of Mercury. Bearer of the Scales of Justice. *St. Januarius.'* And we know of *Janus,* the old Roman guardian of gates and doors, patron of the month of January which was sacred to him, with all 'beginnings.'

Janus faced two ways, as doors and gates opened and shut. Here in this room, we had our exits and our entrances. I have noted too, the four sides of the room, and touched on the problem of the fourth dimensional: the 'additional dimension attributed to space by a hypothetical speculation' is the somewhat comic dictionary definition. Old Janus was guardian of the seasons too, that time-sequence of the four quarters of the year. Thoth was the original measurer, the Egyptian prototype of the later Greek Hermes. I made the connecting link with the still later Roman Mercury, our Flying Dutchman.

For myself, there was a story I loved; I had completely 'forgotten' it; now it is suddenly recalled. The story was about an old light-house keeper called Captain January and a shipwrecked child.

We have only just begun our researches, our 'studies,' the old Professor and I.

78

THIS IS ONLY a beginning but I learned recently (again from Dr. Crow) that 'the seal of the Hippocratic University bears the Tau-cross, entwined with the serpent – exactly the figure used by early Christian artists to represent the serpent which Moses lifted up in the wilderness.' My serpent-and-thistle motive obviously bears some hidden relation to this.

It was Asklepios of the Greeks who was called the *blameless physician.* He was the son of the sun, Phoebos Apollo, and music and medicine were alike sacred to this source of light. This half-man, half-god (Fate decreed) went a little too far when he began actually to raise the dead. He was blasted by the thunder-bolt of an avenging deity, but Apollo, over-riding his father's anger, placed Asklepios among the stars. Our Professor stood this side of the portal. He did not pretend to bring back the dead who had already crossed the threshold. But he raised from dead hearts and stricken minds and maladjusted bodies a host of living children.

One of these children was called Mignon. Not my name certainly. It is true I was small for my age, *mignonne;* but I was not, they said, pretty and I was not, it was very easy to see, quaint and quick and clever like my brother. My brother? Am I my brother's keeper? It appears so. A great many of these brothers fell on the fields of France, in that first war. A great many have fallen since. Numberless poised, disciplined, and valiant young winged Mercuries have fallen from the air, to join the great host of the dead. Leader of the Dead? That was Hermes of the Greeks who took the attribute from Thoth of the Egyptians. The *T* or Tau-cross became caduceus with twined serpents, again corresponding to the *T* or Tau-cross that Moses lifted in the desert.

Am I my brother's keeper? So far as my undisciplined thoughts permit me . . . and further than my disciplined ones can take me. For the Professor was not always right. He did not know – or did he? – that I looked at the things in his room before I looked at him; for I knew the things in his room were symbols of Eternity and contained him then, as Eternity contains him now.

79

THIS OLD JANUS, this beloved light-house keeper, old Captain January, shut the door on transcendental speculations or at least transferred this occult or hidden symbolism to the occult or hidden regions of the personal reactions, dreams, thought associations or thought 'transferences' of the individual human mind. It was the human individual that concerned him, its individual reactions to the problems of every-day, the relation of the child to its environment, its friends, its teachers, above all its parents. As to what happened, after this life was over . . . we as individuals, we as members of one race, one brotherhood of body that contained many different, individual branches, had profited so little by the illuminating teaching of the Master who gave his name to our present era, that it was well for a Prophet, in the old tradition of Israel, to arise, to slam the door on visions of the future, of the after-life, to stand himself like the Roman Centurion before the gate at Pompeii who did not move from his station before the gateway since he received no orders to do so, and who stood for later generations to wonder at, embalmed in hardened lava, preserved in the very fire and ashes that had destroyed him.

'At least, they have not burnt me at the stake.' Did the Professor say that of himself or did someone else say it of him? I think he himself said it. But it was a near-miss . . . even literally . . . and last night, here in London, there were the familiar siren-shrieks, the alerts, each followed by its even more ear-piercing and soul-shattering 'all-clear,' which coming as a sort of aftermath or after-birth of the actual terror is the more devastating. Released from the threat of actual danger, we have time to think about it. And the 'alerts' and the 'all-clears' are punctuated by sound of near or far explosions, at three in the morning, after seven and at lesser intervals . . . the war is not yet over. *Eros* and *Death,* those two were the chief subjects – in fact, the only subjects – of the Professor's eternal pre-occupation. They are still gripped, struggling in the dead-lock. Hercules struggled with Death and is still struggling. But the Professor himself proclaimed the Herculean power of Eros and we know that it was written from the beginning that Love is stronger than Death.

It was the very love of humanity that caused the Professor to stand guardian at the gate. Belief in the soul's survival, in a life after death, wrote the Professor, was the last and greatest fantasy, the gigantic wish-fulfillment that had built up, through the ages, the elaborate and detailed picture of an after-life. He may even have believed this. If so, it was proof again of his Centurion courage. He would stand guardian, he would turn the whole stream of consciousness back into useful, into *irrigation* channels, so that none of this power be wasted. He would clean the Augean stables, he would tame the Nemean lion, he would capture the Erymanthian boar, he would clear the Stymphalian birds from the marshes of the unconscious mind. These things must be done. He indicated certain ways in which they might be done. Until we have completed our twelve labors, he seemed to reiterate, we (mankind) have no right to rest on cloud-cushion fantasies and dreams of an after-life.

From the reasoning upper layers of the thinking mind, he would shut off this dream of heaven, this hope of eternal life. Someone writes somewhere of Sigmund Freud's courageous pessimism. He had little hope for the world. He knew why people laughed at his first findings, at his *Interpretation of Dreams,* his *Delusion and Dream,* and the rest of them. He answered his first ribald detractors with his essay on wit and humor – I think it is impossible to assess this or appreciate it in the translation – but even a superficial observer of his manner of approach to his antagonists would have to grant that the foil of his wit, given a worthy adversary to measure it by, would have none to rival it. He did not wish to prove people *wrong,* he wanted only to show them the way and show them that others had imposed ideas on them that might eventually prove destructive. He even wrote a later, reasoned, calm, and dispassionate essay on the causes for the resurging hatred of the Jews.

80

THERE WAS another Jew who said, *the kingdom of heaven is within you.* He said: *unless you become as little children you shall not enter into the kingdom of heaven.*

81

Others abide our question. Thou art free.
We ask and ask – Thou smilest and art still,
Out-topping knowledge. For the loftiest hill,
Who to the stars uncrowns his majesty,

Planting his steadfast footsteps in the sea,
Making the heaven of heavens his dwelling-place,
Spares but the cloudy border of his base
To the foil'd searching of mortality;

And thou, who didst the stars and sunbeams know,
Self-school'd, self-scann'd, self-honour'd, self-secure,
Didst tread on earth unguess'd at. – Better so!

All pains the immortal spirit must endure,
All weakness which impairs, all griefs which bow,
Find their sole speech in that victorious brow.

I was impelled (almost compelled) to copy this out. It is, of
course, Matthew Arnold's familiar sonnet to Shakespeare. I
had not intended to include it in these notes, but perhaps my
subconscious or unconscious mind recognized an intellectual
family-likeness in 'that victorious brow.' And in this very last
line, there is a sort of Elizabethan conceit or posy, a hidden
reference – a purely personal finding, but for our purpose curiously compelling. We have *victorious* or victory, *Sieg,* and the
sole *voice,* the voice, or speech, or utterance, *Mund,* Sigmund.
There is this, this sonnet, as if written for us, for this occasion,
for this memoir and there is the more personal lyric of the German poet, Goethe, to which I have referred earlier in these
notes. I cannot recall the musical setting – not Schumann's –
that I and a group of my contemporaries sang as school-children. But about the Professor, there was music certainly;
there was music in every syllable he uttered and there was
music implicit in his name, the *Sieg-mund,* the victorious voice
or utterance. There had been music everywhere in Vienna,
there was Beethoven, surcharged and tortured with his sym-
phonies, Mozart, frail and impeccable and deserted and early
dead. There was Schumann, of course, and Schubert's name
was especially associated with the village or suburb of Grin-
zing, not far from Döbling where the Professor had his sum-
mer-quarters that first year I was in Vienna. There was the
city acclaimed by the world as the heart and center of music
and music-lovers. And here was the master-musician, he, too,

a son of Apollo, who would harmonize the whole human spirit, who like Orpheus, would charm the very beasts of the unconscious or subconscious mind, and enliven the dead sticks and stones of buried thoughts and memories.

82

'By chance or intention,' I began these notes on September 19th, a day sacred to Thoth and later to St. Januarius, a name affiliated with that of the Roman Janus, patron of gate-ways and portals, guardian of all 'beginnings.' I did not consciously select this date, though, as I glance at the calendar from time to time, my subconscious mind might have guided me to it. But by quite definite 'intention,' I will finish these 'beginnings,' as for November 2nd, the day of the lighting of the candles for the souls of the Dead.

This is the evening of All Hallows, Halloween; so tomorrow is the first of November 1944, All Saints Day. The angel Michael of the old dispensation, the archangel Michael of the Revelation, is regent of the planet still called Mercury. And in Renaissance paintings, we are not surprised to see Saint Michael wearing the winged sandals and sometimes even the winged helmet of the classic messenger of the Gods. But for the Professor, I choose rather the day following All Saints Day. He was more interested in souls than saints.

83

One of these souls was called Mignon, though its body did not fit it very well. It was small, *mignonne,* though it was not pretty, they said. It was a girl between two boys; but, ironically, it was wispy and mousy, while the boys were glowing and gold. It was not pretty, they said. Then they said it was pretty – but suddenly, it shot up like a weed. They said, surprised, 'She is really very pretty, but isn't it a pity she's so tall?' The soul was called Mignon, but, clearly, it did not fit its body.

But it found itself in a song. Only the tune is missing.

84

IN THE LAST verse of this lyric of Johann Wolfgang Goethe is the line,

Es stürzt der Fels,

the rock breaks or falls in ruins, and indeed this is our very present predicament; but

und über ihn die Flut

following, gives the impression of a living river; though 'and over it the flood' is the literal rendering. Ruins and the flood, but there remains our particular Ark or Barque – a canoe, I called it – that may, even yet, carry us through the seething channels to safe harbor. The Mignon of Goethe's lyric herself joins us in our ritual of question and answer. There were the question marks, as I called them, the series of the imperfect, reversed *S* of the scroll-pattern of the writing-on-the-wall in the Greek island of Corfu, in the spring of the year 1920. There was the *S* or the serpent of my original corner-stone, the enigmatic symbol that a childhood friend, my first 'live' poet, Ezra Pound, translated for me. There was the *S* as serpent, companion to the thistle, the symbol that suggests waste places and the desert; but we have been told that *the desert shall blossom as the rose,* and it was in the desert that Moses raised the standard, the old *T* or Tau-cross of Thoth of the Egyptians. The Professor had been working on a continuation of his 'Moses, the Egyptian' theme, though we had not actually discussed this when I had my 'real' dream of the Egyptian Princess. The Professor asked me then if I were the child Miriam who in the Doré picture had stood, half-hidden in the river-reeds, watching over the new-born child who was to become leader of a captive people and founder of a new religion. Miriam? Mignon?

85

SHE ASKS THE question. Each verse of the lyric is a question or a series of questions. Do you know the Land? Do you know the House? Do you know the Mountain?

Kennst du den Berg und seinen Wolkensteg?

'Do you know the mountain and its cloud-bridge?' is an awkward enough translation but the idea of mountain and bridge is so very suitable to this whole *translation* of the Professor and our work together. *Steg* really means a plank; *foot-bridge* is the more accurate rendering. It is not a bridge for a great crowd of people, and it is a bridge flung, as it were, across the abyss, not built and hammered and constructed. There is plenty of psychoanalytic building and constructing; there are the Gods that some people read Goods. We are dealing here with the realm of fantasy and imagination, flung across the abyss, and these are a poet's lines. The same poet's following lines seem peculiarly appropriate to our subject:

Das Maultier sucht im Nebel seinen Weg,

'The donkey seeks his way in the mist.' There are plenty of donkeys who have set foot on the lower, more easily demarked path-ways of this mountain. Too heavily burdened with intellectual equipment or blinded with the blinkers of prejudice, they go round and round in circles and come back to the stable shaking their heads sadly over their own past folly and the greater folly of the mountain that has so beguiled them. But there are other donkeys who plod on – faithful donkeys. They find their prototype in the Christmas manger-scene.

And our very Phobia is here and the host of allied Phobias, the Dragon and its swarm of children, the Hydra-headed monster, the subject of another of the twelve labors of Hercules.

In Höhlen wohnt der Drachen alte Brut,

the old dragon-brood – or the ancient brood of the Dragon – lives in the caves. Like the Christian of the Puritan poet, John Bunyan, we must push on, through and past these perils. *Kennst du ihn wohl?* Do you actually know this and all these things? If anyone ever did, it is the old Professor. And it was finally St. Michael – wasn't it? – who cast out that aboriginal old Beast? Thoth, Hermes, Mercury, and last Michael, Captain or Centurion of the hosts of heaven.

But it is with the soul rather than with saints and angels that we are concerned; Miriam or Mignon, we may call her.

Kennst du das Land, wo die Zitronen blühn?

'Do you know the land where the orange-tree blossoms?' It was on a winter day that the Professor handed me a branch from an orange-tree with dark laurel-like leaves.

Im dunkeln Laub die Gold-Orangen glühn.

Against the dark leaves is that glow of orange-gold.

Ein sanfter Wind vom blauen Himmel weht;

Yes, it was dark and cold and there was the rumbling of war-chariots from the near horizon. But upon the old Professor and this particular soul, a soft wind blew from a cloudless sky – so gentle was the wind that the myrtle, that with the rose is sacred to Love, did not flutter a leaf, and the laurel grew very tall there.

Die Myrte still und hoch der Lorbeer steht.

It is all there; the lyrical interrogation and the implication that the answer is given with it. It is: do you know the Land – but you do know it, don't you? The House? The Mountain? It is a strange land, a foreign land, a land of classic associations, the myrtle of Aphrodite and the laurel of Apollo. You do know the House, don't you? The roof of the house stood on pillars, like the original roof or part-roof of the temple of Karnak or the Parthenon of Athens. But this house seems nearer in time; there is the great entrance room or *Saal* with its glowing lamps and candles, and beyond it is the brightly tapestried or painted inner room or rooms, the *Gemach* or apartment. It is there that we find the statues, the *Marmorbilder,* even as I had found the little images in the room beyond the actual consulting room, on the Professor's table. The statues stare and stare and seem to say, what has happened to you?

Was hat man dir, du armes Kind, getan?

Poor child, poor shivering and unprotected soul. But – you do know it? – but of course you do. I want to go there with you, O my Guardian (O my Protector), *mit dir, o mein Beschützer, ziehn.*

The land or country, the house, the mountain – we may rest in the garden, we may be sheltered within that house; it is so beautiful; it makes me think of the *Ca d'Oro,* the Golden House on the Grand Canal in Venice. It is the *domus aurea* of the Laurentian litany, and the whole poem in its symbolism follows the cycle of the soul's progress. The garden, the house or hall, the mountain. The mountain is very high for it is crowned like Olympus with clouds, but there is the *Wolkensteg,* the cloud-bridge or foot-way. It is not a very wide bridge, the chasms or gulfs where the ancient dragon lives are deep and terrifying. (But *we have tunneled very deep,* said the old Professor.) Scattered rocks and ruins lie about us and the threatening roar of the cataract is still echoing in our ears. But you, of all people, know it, don't you, the inquiring soul asks; while the plodding little donkey continues its way in the mist. O, let's go away together, pleads the soul, the Mignon of the poet Goethe; let's go, O my dearest, she says first,

o mein Geliebter,

then O my guardian, my protector,

o mein Beschützer,

and in the end, she does not ask if she may go; or exclaim, if only we could go; but there is the simple affirmation, with the white roses – or the still whiter gardenias, as it happened – of uttermost veneration.

Dahin! Dahin
Geht unser Weg! o Vater, lass uns ziehn!

London
September 19, 1944
November 2, 1944

ADVENT

ADVENT

1

MARCH 2, 1933

I CRIED TOO HARD . . . went to the old wooden restaurant with the paintings, like the pictures that my mother did, Swiss scenes, mountains, chalet halfway up a hill, torrent under a bridge. As in her sequence, there were several mid-Victorian snow-scenes here, too. The old plates of the saw-mills, the Lehigh River, summer-house with trellis, deer-park of the Seminary where her father was principal for many years, suggest some near-affiliation with these weathered oils. There are a few still-life studies, apples with a brown jug and the usual bunched full double-peonies with a stalk of blue delphinium, such as we see in the Galleries, but these pictures are homely or home-y, of no intrinsic value.

My mother and I visited an Austrian village, like these pictures; it was in the early summer of 1913 after we had left Italy. My father had returned to America, he said, 'to buy a pair of shoes.' There was a Passion Play; I remember my mother talking on a wooden bridge to one of the village women who said Judas was the fish-man. My mother spoke perfect German. We stayed at an inn; all I remember is the waitress calling me a *backfisch* and our delight in framed color-prints of the old Austrian emperor and the empress in blue décolleté with pearls. That was probably Innsbruck. The village – I don't remember its name – took the visitors into their own homes, wooden cottages or chalets (like these in the weathered paintings), and there was a rather overwhelming feeling of the wood-carved Christ at corners of the village and at the entrance to the old bridge.

I wandered alone across the bridge but did not get far. The forest seemed menacing.

At Christmas time, we had deer on the moss under the tree. Our grandfather made us clay sheep.

I cried too hard . . . I do not know what I remembered: the hurt of the cold, nun-like nurses at the time of my first London confinement, spring 1915; the shock of the *Lusitania* going down just before the child was still-born; fear of drowning; young men on park benches in blue hospital uniform; my father's anti-war sentiments and his violent *volte-face* in 1918; my broken marriage; a short period with friends in Cornwall in 1918; my father's telescope, my grandfather's microscope. If I let go (I, this one drop, this one ego under the microscope-telescope of Sigmund Freud) I fear to be dissolved utterly.

I had what Bryher called the 'jelly-fish' experience of double ego; bell-jar or half-globe as of transparent glass spread over my head like a diving-bell and another manifested from my feet, so enclosed I was for a short space in St. Mary's, Scilly Isles, July 1918, immunized or insulated from the war disaster. But I could not stay in it; I re-materialized and Bryher took me to Greece in the spring of 1920.

My older brother and I took our father's magnifying glass, and he showed me how to 'burn paper.' Our father stopped us as he found it dangerous, 'playing with fire.'

When I told Professor Freud I was married in 1913, he said, 'Ah, twenty years ago.'

Sigmund Freud is like a curator in a museum, surrounded by his priceless collection of Greek, Egyptian, and Chinese treasures; he is 'Lazarus stand forth'; he is like D. H. Lawrence, grown old but matured and with astute perception. His hands are sensitive and frail. He is midwife to the soul. He is himself the soul. Thought of him bashes across my forehead, like a death-head moth; he is not the sphinx but the sphinx-moth, the death-head moth.

No wonder I am frightened. I let death in at the window. If I do not let ice-thin window-glass intellect protect my soul or my emotion, I let death in.

But perhaps I will be treated with a psychic drug, will take away a nameless precious phial from his cavern. Perhaps I will learn the secret, be priestess with power over life and death.

He beat on my pillow or the head-piece of the old couch I lie on. He was annoyed with me. His small chow, Yofi, sits at his feet. We make an ancient cycle or circle, wise-man, woman, lioness (as he calls his chow)!

He is a Jew; like the last Prophet, he would break down the old law of Leviticus: death by stoning for the vagrant, and unimaginable punishment for the lawless. The old Victorian law is hard; Havelock Ellis and Sigmund Freud tempered it for my generation.

Kenneth Macpherson called me 'recording angel.' I will endeavor to record the grain in the painted apple, in the painted basket, hanging to the left of the wooden dresser, directly in line with my eyes, as I glance up from my note-book. The painting is dimmed by smoke and winter damp, but there must be black seeds in the painted apples, there must be white wine in the painted jug. I wanted to paint like my mother, though she laughed at her pictures we admired so.

My father went out of doors; the stars commanded him. Human souls command Sigmund Freud.

In Corfu, spring 1920, among my many fantasies, I imagined a figure came in sack-cloth; he was not in appearance the conventional Messiah, though his words made me think he was Christ. He said, 'You were once kind to one of my people.' To whom was I kind?

There was a Russian-American Jew, John Cournos or Ivan Ivanovitch Korshun, as he said his name was. I don't think Korshun is the right spelling, but he pronounced it like that and as I remember, he said Korshun meant a hawk.

There was another, a Mr. Brashaer, a famous lens-maker who fitted the lenses to my father's Zenith telescope. Was this the lens I imagined in the Scilly Isles, or the two convex lenses that I called bell-jars?

I came back from Aegina, from the Hellenic Cruise trip of spring 1932. My daughter was with me; she was just thirteen. I came back from Egypt, 1923, at the time of the Tutankhamen excavations; I came back from the Ionian Islands in 1920.

I saw the world through my double-lens; it seemed everything had broken but that. I watched snow-flakes through a magnified pane of glass.

Who was this that I had been kind to? Mr. Brashaer was small, dark, vivid. He was a famous lens-maker, the most famous in America, perhaps the most famous in the world. He is small in my imagination, this person I was kind to. Is this the magic *homunculus* of the alchemists?

2

FREUD TOOK ME into the other room and showed me the things on his table. He took the ivory Vishnu with the upright serpents and canopy of snake heads, and put it into my hands. He selected a tiny Athené from near the end of the semicircle, he said, 'This is my favorite.' The Vishnu was set in the center with the statues arranged either side; there is an engraving of the Professor somewhere, seated at this desk behind or within the circle. He opened the case against the wall and displayed his treasures, antique rings.

We spoke of fees; he said, 'Do not worry about that, that is my concern.' He went on, 'I want you to feel at home.' Then he said he thought my voice was 'delicate' and added, as if there might be danger of my letting outside matters intrude, 'I am, after all, seventy-seven.'

I found I was not so shy. I told him of Miss Chadwick and of how I had suffered, during my preliminary sessions with her, spring 1931. I would deliberately assemble all the sorry memories in my effort to get at the truth. He said, 'We never know what is important or what is unimportant until after.' He said, 'We must be impartial, see fair play to ourselves.'

I told him how the first impression of his room had over-whelmed and upset me. I had not expected to find him sur-rounded by these treasures, in a museum, a temple. We talked of Egypt. I spoke of the yellow sand, the blue sky, the beetle-scarabs. Then I said that Egypt was a series of living Bible illustrations and I told him of my delight in our Gustave Doré, as a child.

He said how fortunate I had been to discover reality 'super-imposed' (his word) on the pictures.

I had told him in my last sessions of the Princess and the baby in the basket.

He asked me again if I was Miriam or saw Miriam, and did I think the Princess was actually my mother?

He said a dream sometimes showed a 'corner,' but I argued that this dream was a finality, an absolute, or a synthesis. Nor was I, as he had suggested in the first instance, the baby, the 'founder of a new religion.' Obviously it was he, who was that light out of Egypt.

But it is true that we play puss-in-a-corner, find one angle and another or see things from different corners or sides of a room. Yes, we play hide-and-seek, hunt-the-slipper, and hunt-the-thimble and patiently and meticulously patch together odds and ends of our picture-puzzle. We spell words upside down and backward and crosswise, for our crossword puzzle, and then again we run away and hide in the cellar or the attic or in our mother's clothes-closet. We play magnificent charades.

But the Professor insisted I myself wanted to be Moses; not only did I want to be a boy but I wanted to be a hero. He suggested my reading Otto Rank's *Der Mythus von der Geburt des Helden*.

MARCH 3, FRIDAY

Remembering Vishnu, I think the ivory is like a half-lily.

I do not know if the white lily was a fantasy, dream, or reality.

I stood looking through the iron railing of the garden, surrounded by a crowd of small boys of assorted ages, brothers no doubt, smaller cousins and the neighboring bandits.

A very old, tall old man is wandering in the garden. With him, there is a younger edition of himself, but the tall young man is the gardener.

The grandfather, godfather, god-the-father sees the children. He summons them to the iron fence. He looks them over. But only *one* is chosen.

The very small girl staggers forward, overcome, shy yet bold. She crosses the threshold. She stands on the garden path. It is a 'real' garden, with sandy path like our grandfather's garden; it is shut in, however; it is not a very large garden, it is more like a long unroofed room between the house walls. There are trees in the garden, ordinary trees, real trees.

She can only distinguish trees at this time by their fruit or blossom. But these are ordinary trees, in the ordinary time of summer-leaf.

The old gentleman says that she must choose what she wants. Actually, there is no pansy border to 'pick' from and no fruit on the trees. But she must choose what she wants.

She sees what she wants. Is it the only flower in this garden?

It is not a flower she would have chosen, for she would never have been allowed to choose it. It is an Easter-lily or Madonna-lily, growing by the path.

She points to it, overwhelmed by her audacity.

The gardener unclasps a knife, cuts off the flower for her.

But this is rather overwhelming; what does one do with one huge Easter-lily? She races down the now empty street to their front door on Church Street.

She rushes into their front sitting room or parlor. It seems emptier than usual, with light falling from the apparently uncurtained windows. There is mama sewing, there is mamalie sewing.

My Easter-lily!

'Ah,' says mama or says mamalie (our grandmother), 'that will look beautiful on your grandfather's new grave.'

She is alone at Nisky Hill, where her grandfather has recently been buried. There is just this one mound, like a flower-bed. She 'plants' the lily.

Obviously, this is my inheritance. I derive my imaginative faculties through my musician-artist mother, through her part-Celtic mother, through the grandfather of English and middle-European extraction. My father was pure New England, a one-remove pioneer to Indiana, who returned 'back east.' My father is here too, but dissolved or resolved into the 'other grandfather,' whom we had never known. My mother's father was the first 'dead' person I had ever known. I do not at the time actually associate the godfather or god-the-father with a recognizable personality. He is a stranger. He is a General from the Old South. I later ask my mother where he has gone? But there is no such person, no General from the Old South, no such house with a narrow walled-in garden, she says, on Church Street. She knows everyone on Church Street.

I do not accept this, but I cannot not find the house, opposite what had been the College; they are tearing down the College and putting up new buildings but anyhow, the old godfather's house was the other side of the street. It does not quite work out, but it is only afterwards, long afterwards, that I find this out.

The trees were very leafy. He gives me an Easter-lily. Easter-lilies come at Easter time, spring or early spring; the trees are summer trees in full leaf. But worse than that. It was after he gave her the lily, only a day or two later, that he sends his sleigh. It is a beautiful sleigh with sleigh-bells. The gardener is the coachman. There is a thick fur rug. We drive across the untrodden snow; there is no one in the streets.

He sent a message with the coachman. He said he had sent the sleigh because of the little girl. 'When will he come again?' I ask my mother. Is it winter, summer? 'Why – what?' 'The sleigh, of course, he said he would send it whenever I wanted, it is for you and me and Gilbert and Harold, but he said it was because of me that we could all ride in his sleigh.'

We were all tucked up together under the fur rug.

But no one had sent us a sleigh, my mother told me.

Anyhow, the seasons are all wrong.

In Corfu, someone placed two white lilies and one red tulip on my table. Bryher probably. But there seemed mystery about it. I did not ask Bryher about it. I had learned long ago not to inquire too deeply into the mystery.

The ivory Vishnu sits upright in his snake-hood, like the piston of a calla-lily, or a jack-in-the-pulpit.

My grandfather was the jack-in-the-pulpit, a pastor or clergyman.

Church Street was our street, the Church was our Church. It was founded by Count Zinzendorf who named our town Bethlehem.

People tell one things, and other children laugh at one's ignorance. 'But Jesus was not born *here*.'

That may be true. We will not discuss the matter. Only

after some forty years, we approach it. 'I don't know if I dreamed this or if I just imagined it, or if later I imagined that I dreamed it.' 'It does not matter,' he said, 'whether you dreamed it or imagined it or whether you just made it up, this moment. I do not think you would deliberately falsify your findings. The important thing is that it shows the trend of your fantasy or imagination.'

He goes on, 'You were born in Bethlehem? It is inevitable that the Christian myth –' He paused. 'This does not offend you?' 'Offend me?' 'My speaking of your religion in terms of myth,' he said. I said, 'How could I be offended?' 'Bethlehem is the town of Mary,' he said.

3

MARCH 4

I WAS COLD and I found difficulty in starting. I went on talking about the Doré pictures, the dead baby in the *Judgment of Solomon*. I told him of the graves of my two sisters. I had never known these sisters; one was a half-sister and really belonged to the two grown half-brothers, Eric and Alfred. Their mother was there too. We went on with the lily-fantasy. The old man was obviously, he said, God.

, The lily was the Annunciation-lily. I said it was the ivory Vishnu that had prompted me to tell the anecdote. He asked me about my early religious background. I said it was not that they were strict, we were not often punished. I remembered, however, terrible compulsions or premonitions of punishment. Hell from the Bible stories seemed a real place. But I did not speak of this. I went on to tell him of our Christmas candles.

'An atmosphere . . .' he said.

He said, 'There is no more significant symbol than a lighted candle. You say you remember your grandfather's Christmas-Eve service? The girls as well as the boys had candles?' It seemed odd that he should ask this.

Sigmund Freud got up from his chair at the back of the couch, and came and stood beside me. He said, 'If every child had a lighted candle given, as you say they were given at your grandfather's Christmas Eve service, by the grace of God, we would have no more problems. . . . That is the true heart of all religion.'

Later at home, in bed, I was stricken and frightened, thinking of all the things that I wanted or rather felt impelled to tell him. I think of Sigmund Freud as this little-papa, Papalie, the grandfather. Talking half-asleep to myself, or rather to the Professor, I realize I am using the rhythm or language I use only for cats and children. There is my daughter's cat, Peter, that, she tells me, 'I have left to you in my will.'

'It's an old, old cat,' I say, talking to the Professor, and then it occurs to me that the jerk of his elbow as he orders or summons me from his waiting room to the consulting room is like the angular flap of a bird-wing. I have lately been watching these great crows or rooks here in the gardens off the Ringstrasse.

Yes, there is a singular finality about his least remark, his most insignificant gesture. There is the Pallas Athené on his desk, beyond the double door, leading from the consulting room to the inner sanctum. *Just above my chamber door* – that was a bust of Pallas, if I am not mistaken, from Poe's *Raven*. There is a *quoth-the-Raven* mystery about his every utterance, though he seems to huddle rather than to perch, more like an old owl, *hibou sacré*, in the corner back of the couch.

I remember a special gift from my father: this time the gift is not from little-papa, Papalie. The wretched and fascinating creature stared and stared at me, from the top of his bookshelf. The bookshelf ran the length of the wall opposite his table, or rather there were bookcases along all the walls that were not broken by windows. I must have been indeed the child of heroes and a hero from *Geburt des Helden*, for I asked him, 'May I have that white owl?'

It was an extremely large owl. It was very white. It lived under a bell-jar, it had large unblinking gold or amber eyes. I was suddenly reminded of the golden fur of the little Yofi lioness. If my grandfather gave me a lighted candle, my father gave me a snow-owl.

True, there was a qualification about this miracle, as there so often is in a true fairy tale. Yes, the owl was mine; it was mine for ever, he would not ask me to give it back to him. He had reproved one of us one day for being an 'Indian-giver.' Someone rashly gave away a bag of marbles, a cock-a-doodle-do trumpet (a rooster of *papier mâché* whose head was like a Halloween false-face), or Joey from the Punch and Judy. Though individually the dolls were divided, the 'show' was common property. There was a snag about some gift. 'What is an Indian-giver?' 'It is someone who gives something and asks for it back again.' But he wasn't an Indian-giver. I could keep the snow-owl.

There was, however, this condition. I had told the Professor of the snow-owl. I told him there was one condition, and paused as if to emphasize the drama.

But perhaps it is an old trick.

The Professor said before I had time to tell him, 'Ah – yes – he gave the owl to you, on the condition that it stayed where it was.'

But as I lie here, in my comfortable bed, in the Hotel

Regina, I go on with my reverie. I am not preparing for tomorrow's session, I am simply going on with today's. By some curious freak of luck, a gardener brought me the tip of a cactus plant, to plant in a flower pot, in pebbles and sand. 'Do not water it, it will grow best, right out in the sun; I have a huge plant, a tree really,' he told me. The gardener explained that he had grown his cactus tree from a slip just like the one he brought me. I was proud of my cactus plant and moved it about in the sun. It would grow into a tree.

It really wasn't fair.

My three-inch strip of tough cactus fiber began to glow, it did not grow, it simply burst into a huge flower. It was like a red water-lily. Its petals were smooth and cold, though they should have been blazing. Well, perhaps they were. I thought the gardener would be so pleased. He said, 'I have had my plant now for years and not a sign of a blossom.'

It wasn't fair.

There was no rivalry about the butterfly, but that wasn't fair either. For some reason, this giant worm had chosen a rather fragile stalk from my garden plot to build on. It may have been that the packets of our 'cheap seeds' had been badly sifted or assorted and that some strange exotic had got in among them. But how did the worm get there? There was only one of the nicotiana plants. I broke off the stem and put it with what tobacco-flower leaves were left and placed the cocoon where I felt it would be safest, on the top of my father's bookcase. The owl was one end, the other end was the Indian skull, at least we called it an Indian skull. It had been dug up or plowed up by him or by his father when our father was a boy in Indiana.

I know that I am in bed in the Regina Hotel, Freiheitsplatz, Vienna. I know that it is March 4, 1933. I am not sure but I think that this is my father's birthday. He never wanted a 'birthday' in our house, that seemed every other week to mark some festivity in mama's or Mamalie's Birthday Book or Text Book. I think this is my father's birthday. He was younger than the Professor when he died, so perhaps it is natural, one way and another, to give the Professor the rôle of grand- or great-father, for all he is little-father or Papalie.

If I tell the Professor about the cactus *and* the butterfly, he will think I have made up one or the other, or both.

As I say, it was not quite fair, for I had had some slight converse with amateur experts, though I myself knew the name of not one butterfly. The thing that hatched out was a moth. It was exotic and enormous. It was literally the size of a not-so-small bird. It crawled or fluttered the length of the top shelf and settled on the Indian skull that my father or my grand-father had dug or plowed up when my father was a boy in Indiana.

My father and I agreed there was nothing to be done about it but to open the window and hope that it would fly out.

There is a bed-lamp, on the stand at my elbow. There is, I remember, a flattering soft-rose lamp-shade. If I switch on the light, I will see the length of green curtains, the comfortable green-upholstered arm-chair, glass-topped dressing-table, and the ordinary table with my books and papers.

I will have to switch on the light soon, for my eyes, staring into darkness, wonder if again I crossed the threshold. No, I am sure about the cactus. I am not quite sure about the butterfly.

I was wrong about the butterfly. I did not break off a heavy cocoon, but I gathered the enormous green caterpillar with the tobacco-flower stalk and placed the stalk and worm in a cardboard box. Did I cut holes in the box? There was ventilation somewhere. This was my own worm.

In the box, among the fresh green tobacco leaves, and the old brown tobacco leaves, he wove his huge cocoon.

How did he get out of the box? Did I hear him scratching? Did he flutter and beat his wings against the box?

How did I get the cardboard box onto the top of the tall bookcase? Did I climb up on a chair? I was not tall enough to reach the top shelf, even with a chair.

Did I make it all up? Did I dream it? And if I dreamt it, did I dream it forty years ago, or did I dream it last night?

It was the huge green caterpillar that I gathered with the blossoming nicotiana.

I am wrong about my father's birthday. My father's birthday is in November.

Why did I say today, March 4th, is my father's birthday?

4

HIBOU SACRÉ! I asked him how he was and he smiled a charming, wrinkled smile that reminded me of D. H. Lawrence. He told me (in French) how Napoleon's mother used to say, even at the height of his fame, 'That is all right as long as it lasts.' I spoke of the last war-year. He said he had reason to remember the epidemic, as he lost his favorite daughter. 'She is here,' he said, and he showed me a tiny locket that he wore, fastened to his watch-chain. She had died of the epidemic in Hamburg, though the baby she had just had survived. I remembered Dr. Sachs speaking of this girl, 'the beautiful Sophie.'

So the beautiful Sophie died, having her child about the same time as I was having mine, early spring 1919. I had the same Spanish influenza and though it was common knowledge that in no instance did both child and mother live after the depletion of pneumonia, yet I was the miraculous exception. It was not the child nor my critical physical condition that caused the final collapse.

But there was so much to tell. I dodged the actual details of my desolation and told the Professor how kind Havelock Ellis had been to me when I saw him in his flat in Brixton, those few times before the birth of my child. I had written to Dr. Ellis, although Daphne Bax who had arranged for me to stay in a cottage near her in Buckinghamshire, during the winter of 1919, had tried to discourage any idea of my meeting Havelock Ellis whom I so greatly admired. Mrs. Ellis had had a house at one time in Buckinghamshire, near Daphne. Daphne said, 'Oh, Havelock – no one ever manages to meet Havelock. He is remote, apart, a recluse, a Titan, a giant.' Perhaps Daphne's so taking things for granted spurred me to approach this Titan. I received a courteous note in answer to my letter to him, and the next time I made the trip from Princes Risborough to London, I went to see this Titan. He served China tea, with a plate of salted pecans and peanuts. There was an unexpected charm and authenticity in his artist décor. He wore a brown velvet smoking-jacket and showed me some of his treasures, a Buddha that his father, a sea captain, had brought back from China, a copy of a famous bust of himself done by – I forget who. There were various autographed photographs of people I had never met but heard of; Walt Whitman among others looked down from the wall. There were Russian cigarettes and Dr. Ellis served lemon, in the Russian or American manner, with the tea. I went on talking to the Professor of the effect that Dr. Ellis had on me; I had expected to meet the rather remote, detached, and much-abused scientist, I found the artist. Sigmund Freud said, 'Ah, you tell this all so beautifully.'

Dr. Ellis was in my fantasies when I went, July 1919, with Bryher to the Scilly Isles. He knew Cornwall and had lived there off and on, for many years in 'retreat' as Daphne would have said, working on his famous volumes. The Scilly Isles, in the flow of the Gulf Stream, suggested the Mediterranean to me. There were great birds; they perched there in 'retreat,' at certain seasons, both from the tropic zones and from the Arctic. It was here at this time I had my 'jelly-fish' experience, as Bryher called it. There were palm-trees, coral-plants, mesambeanthum, opened like water-lilies the length of the grey walls; the sort of fibrous under-water leaf and these open sea-flowers gave one the impression of being submerged.

We were in the little room that Bryher had taken for our study when I felt this impulse to 'let go' into a sort of balloon, or diving-bell, as I have explained it, that seemed to hover over me. There was an old-fashioned sideboard and I remember thinking, 'I must really ask for another jar to put those flowers in.' They had stuck a great bundle of calla-lilies, wedged tight into a jam pot. Two or three of the flower-stalks would have been more effective, with a few of the spear-like leaves. There was an engraving of the inevitable Landseer's *Stag at Bay* over the fireplace, screened now with a ruffle or fan of red paper. When I tried to explain this to Bryher and told her it might be something sinister or dangerous, she said, 'No, no, it is the most wonderful thing I ever heard of. Let it come.'

I tried to write a rough account of this singular adventure, *Notes on Thought and Vision*. There was, I explained to Bryher, a second globe or bell-jar rising as if it were from my feet. I was enclosed. I felt I was safe but seeing things as through water. I felt the double globe come and go and I could have dismissed it at once and probably would have if I had been alone. But it would not have happened, I imagine, if I had been alone. It was being with Bryher that projected the fantasy, and all the time I was thinking that this would be an interesting bit of psychological data for Dr. Havelock Ellis.

When I returned to London, I sent my *Notes* to Dr. Ellis. I thought he would be so interested. But he appeared unsympathetic, or else he did not understand or else he may have thought it was a danger signal.

Dr. Ellis did not understand but the Professor understood perfectly.

As I was leaving, the Professor asked me, 'Are you lonely?' I said, 'Oh – no.'

No, I was not lonely. There were museums, galleries, the walks in the *Stadtpark,* visiting old churches. I scribbled in my notebook, and leafed over magazines and books sent me from London and America. It did not occur to me, until I was back in my bed, that I had omitted to tell the Professor the story of the caterpillar that had so concerned me last night before falling to sleep. Now, I must assemble the picture again.

Where had I left off? There was some snag somewhere. There were, now I recalled, several snags. To begin with, I had got my father's birthday all wrong. Why substitute March for November, but the four was right; yes, I was certain that November 4 was my father's birthday.

That caterpillar? No, it would not scratch and beat with its wings inside the box, for surely when it had woven its shell, I would have left the box-lid off altogether. Why this box and box-lid? There is that rather gruesome old print in the Professor's waiting room, called 'Buried Alive.'

I must have taken fresh leaves one day and found the spun sheath. But how long did it take a caterpillar to weave its elaborate vestment? Why did I forget the caterpillar? Why did I remember it?

There it is on my table, that last volume that I disliked so. It was sent to me from London, another fanatical woman writing her story of D. H. Lawrence. Lawrence? It was in March he died.

Then I substituted my father's birthday for the death-day of D. H. Lawrence.

5

MARCH 5

I HAD SAID, in the beginning, that I only wanted to tell the story, it was like the *Ancient Mariner*, but he did not know or pretended not to know the poem. I had connected the *Ancient Mariner* with the Bible as an uncle had a Doré illustrated edition that we laid flat on the floor, in my grandmother's house, as we did at home our own illustrated Bible, before we could read. I connect Poe and Coleridge in my sequence, as they were both alleged drug-addicts, Poe with his Lenores and haunted Ushers, and Coleridge with his Xanadu, his Kubla Khan. I was publicly reproved at Miss Gordon's school in West Philadelphia, when I was fifteen, because I firmly stated that Edgar Allan Poe was my favorite among American writers. I was told by Miss Pitcher who had otherwise encouraged me, even at that age, in my literary aspirations, that Poe was not a good influence, he was 'unwholesome, morbid.'

Today, lying on the famous psychoanalytical couch, I have a feeling of evaporating cold menthol, some form of ether, laid on my 'morbid' brow. Wherever my fantasies may take me now, I have a center, security, aim. I am centralized or re-oriented here in this mysterious lion's den or Aladdin's cave of treasures.

I am salvaged, saved; ship-wrecked like the Mariner, I have sensed bell-notes from the hermit's chapel. There is Baudelaire too and his *Fleurs du Mal,* but there is no evil in Sigmund Freud. Full fathom five thy father lies, of his bones are coral made, those are pearls that were his eyes, nothing of him that doth fade, but doth suffer a sea-change into something rich and strange, I whisper under my breath, in one of those pregnant pauses, while the fumes of the aromatic cigar waft above me, from the nook in the corner behind my head.

Are we psychic coral-polyps? Do we build one upon another? Did I (sub-aqueous) in the Scilly Isles, put out a feeler? Did I die in my polyp manifestation and will I leave a polyp skeleton of coral to blend with this entire myriad-minded coral chaplet or entire coral island? My psychic experiences were sub-aqueous.

I must remember to tell Sigmund Freud of Norman Douglas' epigram on Havelock Ellis, 'He is a man with one eye in the country of the blind.'

I do not want to talk today. I am drifting out to sea. But I know I am safe, can return at any moment to *terra firma*. Yes, there was a dream last night but the ramifications are too elaborate. I dreamt I sent my book *Hedylus* to Peter Van Eck, whom I met on the boat going to Athens, spring 1920. I will have to tell him about the book, Hedylus the Alexandrian poet who is mentioned in the *Garland of Meleager*, and Hedyle his mother.

I will have to tell him that Bryher came into this dream, disguised at a Halloween party, as a black cat, actually as Peter whom my daughter says she has left me in her will. Puss-in-boots?

No, I could not tell him about *Hedylus*. What had I told him? I had not told him of the caterpillar, that is certain.

I was annoyed with that last book on Lawrence, but it gave me that date. It was March 2nd, not far removed from 4, and 2 x 2 is 4, and will we ever lay a four-square foundation?

Why lay a foundation?

I wasn't fair but I could hardly cope with his enormous novels. They didn't seem to ring true. That is, I was not susceptible to the frenzy in them. In them? Or in the choros of Maenids? I do not like that last book. I have not liked any of these books that have come out since his death. What do they know of Lawrence?

I should talk to the Professor about Lawrence, but I was particularly annoyed by his supercilious references to psychoanalysis and, by implication or inference, to the Professor himself.

The Man Who Died?

I don't remember it, I don't think of it. Only it was a re-statement of his philosophy, but it came too late.

I don't mean that.

I have carefully avoided coming to terms with Lawrence, the Lawrence of *Women in Love* and *Lady Chatterley*.

But there was this last Lawrence.

He did not accept Sigmund Freud, or implied it in his essay.

I don't want to think of Lawrence.

'I hope never to see you again,' he wrote in that last letter.

Then after the death of Lawrence, Stephen Guest brought me the book and said, 'Lawrence wrote this for you.'

Lawrence was imprisoned in his tomb; like the print hanging in the waiting room, he was 'Buried Alive.'

We are all buried alive.

The story comes back automatically when I switch off the bed-lamp.

I do not seem to be able to face the story in the daytime.

Yes, it was abomination. I could see it writhing. 'It's only a caterpillar.' Perhaps I cannot really talk yet. I am seated at one remove from a doll-chair, on the porch. I look down the wide wooden steps. There is the grapevine, as we called it, and leaf-shadows. They are crouched under the grape arbor. I can scream, I can cry. It is not a thing that the mind could possibly assimilate. They are putting salt on the caterpillar and it writhes, huge like an object seen under a microscope, or looming up it is a later film-abstraction.

No, how can I talk about the crucified Worm? I have been leafing over papers in the café, there are fresh atrocity stories. I cannot talk about the thing that actually concerns me, I cannot talk to Sigmund Freud in Vienna, 1933, about Jewish atrocities in Berlin.

MARCH 6, MONDAY

I dream Joan and Dorothy are arguing. Joan possesses herself of some boxes and jewel-cases of mine: she treats my dream treasures as common property, spreads them out on a table. I am angry at her casual appropriation of my personal belongings. I take up one red-velvet-lined box (actually Bryher had got this for me in Florence) and say passionately, 'Can you understand *nothing*?' Joan is a tall girl, we stand level, challenging each other. I say, 'Can't you understand? My *mother* gave me this box.' I press this red-velvet-lined red-leather Florentine box against my heart. Actually, physically, my heart is surcharged and beating wildly at the vehemence of my passion.

I recall the Phoenix symbol of D. H. Lawrence and of how I had thought of the Professor as an owl, hawk, or sphinx-moth. Are these substitutions for the scripture hen gathering her chicks?

My daughter was born the last day of March with *daffodils that come before the swallow dares* out of *The Winter's Tale*. Richard had brought me many daffodils, that English Lent-lily.

I have been reading James Jeans's *Stars in Their Courses*, and am reminded of my bitter disappointment when a well-meaning young uncle called me to the nursery window. 'Look,' he said, 'there is the Bear in the sky.' I blinked from the frosty winter-window. I had been shown the frost-flowers, like stars, in kindergarten. That satisfied me. But here was another wonder. I gazed and blinked but there was no Bear to be seen. When I told this to Dr. Sachs, he said, 'Such a small child would hardly register such a disappointment.' Perhaps I explained it badly. I was shocked that my uncle should deceive me. Surely, a small child would feel the hurt, or the practical joke, feel that a grown-up was playing some trick. I don't know what sort of a Bear I expected to find there, but a white bear, a polar-bear, a snow-bear might not be impossible, as there was (and I knew that) Santa Claus with his reindeer who sped over the roofs of our town on Christmas Eve. We did not see him, of course, for he liked to give us our presents secretly. But the uncle assured me that the Bear was there and he would show me a picture of it.

The Professor has found me a thick rug now, for the couch. He always seems interested when I tell him of my animal findings and fairy-tale associations. At least, it was not my father who deceived me. The Professor said I had not made the conventional transference from mother to father, as is usual with a girl at adolescence. He said he thought my father was a cold man.

But our father took us out one evening in the snow and bought us a box of animals. He divided them afterwards, as we had done with the Punch and Judy dolls. There seemed no friction among the three of us, as to the choice of dolls or later of the animals. My older brother took the elephant of course, I had the elk, the small boy had the polar-bear. I should have liked the bear but we had first choice in order of age, then second choice. I don't remember what our second and our third choice was.

The big boy of course took Punch and I had Judy and the little boy loved Joey. That was all right. Then Gilbert took the policeman of course, I had the beadle, the little boy had – surely there was another doll, I know it worked out. I can't remember the sixth doll – or did we compromise and give him Toby the dog?

The Professor had first written me that he would be ready to see me 'next year, January or February.' This is next year, but we decided to wait, as he said he feared the 'polar-bear weather' might upset me. I remember writing him that I wanted to come in March, whatever the weather might be. Yes – it was in London in March that I heard from America of the death of my father, though he must have died in February. My mother died too in March but eight years later. The word reached me at Riant Château, Territet, where she had been with us, on the first day of spring, 1927.

Again, I feel, lying on this couch that a sort of phosphorescence is evaporating from my forehead and I can almost breathe this anodyne, this ether.

Am I reminded of happy release from pain and the fortunate auspices, predicted for my daughter who arrived in the vernal equinox, and at the high tide of the sun, at noon exactly?

Surely the high tide of her stars brought fortune to me.

Some of these things I touched on with the Professor. I cannot classify the living content of our talks together by recounting them in a logical or textbook manner. It was, as he had said of my grandfather, 'an atmosphere. . . .'

I don't know why I pick on Joan and Dorothy, two devoted friends in London. That is, they are devoted to each other; I am really only an acquaintance. Do I associate them with my aunts? Poor Aunt Laura was so happy when my mother told her, when she visited us in Switzerland, that she could have all her clothes. Joan and Dorothy are substitutes, rivals for my mother's love. It does not matter who they are. We were together in Florence, too. My modest jewels are precious to me, for their association, a string of smoke-sapphires or star-sapphires and a bracelet (from a shop where at one time Cellini had been master silversmith), some leather frames and old paperbacked Tauchnitz editions, rebound in the patterned red-lily parchment paper.

When I switch off my bed-light, I realize that I might have seen Lawrence there.

MARCH 7

I dream of Havelock Ellis with his white beard. We had once talked of old English public houses or pubs as they call them. We go on with this conversation. I don't remember what it led up to, but he talks about the 'doors.' I finally think in my dream, 'He has forgotten I am a woman and do not go into pubs or saloons – men evidently discuss various pubs and pub-doors like this among themselves.' But it is Havelock Ellis, propped up in bed, who has the rôle of the invalid or analysand while I who sit beside him am the analyst.

Then Havelock Ellis becomes the analyst in the Professor's place but, reclining on the couch, I think, 'Havelock Ellis will be bored, he doesn't really care for psychoanalysis nor really know much about it; how can I expect him to be interested or to understand me?' We then seem to go on with the conversation in an ordinary way; he wants to find a French girl 'with a perfect accent.' I say, 'My daughter has a perfect accent.' I wake to realize that someone is rapping – a letter is slipped under my door.

I have been frightened, I do not want to mention blood to the Professor. I opened the front door, ran out to welcome my father in the dark and found blood on his head, dripping . . . This was soon after we moved from Bethlehem to the Flower Observatory, outside Philadelphia. The cause of my father's accident always remained a mystery. He might have slipped off the old-fashioned steam tram or the local train engine might have backfired. We were not allowed to see our father for some days. We were afraid he might be dead. When we finally went to his room he was propped up, as I had imagined Havelock Ellis in the dream, but his hair and beard had turned white. It was another father, wax-pale, a ghost.

I think I was ten years old at that time. I had 'forgotten' this until I began my work with Miss Chadwick.

I had 'forgotten' my father's accident for thirty-five years.

I try to outline in a detached way the story of the three children finding their father. I qualify my terror of death by saying, 'We overheard Mr. Evans, one of our father's assistants at the Observatory, say it was concussion of the brain.' The Professor waved this aside. 'It could not have been concussion,' he said. I did not know whether he was trying to spare me distress, or if he felt I had in some way forced this recital.

Sigmund Freud said at our next session that he saw 'from signs' that I did not want to be analyzed.

I had seen a beautiful etching of him in an art-shop, on the *Ring*.

Today, I went and ordered a copy.

I am sick today, shaken, unnerved, disoriented.

I feel I should discuss my father's accident and the discovery of this submerged, long-delayed shock.

Yes, it is true, he must see my conflict 'from signs.'

How can I tell him of my constant pre-vision of disaster?

It is better to have an unsuccessful or 'delayed' analysis than to bring my actual terror of the lurking Nazi menace into the open.

Yes, I was 'Buried Alive.'

Is this why my thoughts return to Lawrence?

I can only remember that last book he wrote. *The Man Who Died* was buried alive.

MARCH 8, WEDNESDAY

I dream of a photograph of an unbearded D. H. Lawrence. I had such a photograph of my father, taken when he was sixteen or seventeen before he went with his brother to the war. There were daguerreotypes of these two brothers, taken when they were a little younger. The older brother was by far the more attractive. But I looked into the reflecting surface of the silver plate of the younger, and I looked out at myself.

I first met Lawrence in August 1914 at the time of the actual outbreak of war; he looked taller in evening-dress. It was the only time I saw this unbearded manifestation of Lawrence. Richard Aldington said afterwards that Lawrence looked like a soldier in mufti.

In my dream, there is a neat 'professional' woman with Lawrence and there is a group of children. Is the 'professional' woman a sort of secretary? I acted for a short time as secretary to my father.

Lawrence at one time was a school-master and I always had a longing to teach. The children in this dream 'class' or family are of assorted sizes; they stand back of Lawrence and the young woman, grouped round a piano.

My mother taught music and painting at one time, at the old Seminary.

Now the children resolve or dissolve into a picture of a number of models of full-rigged ships.

Havelock Ellis' father was a sea captain and one of my father's textbooks was *Practical Astronomy Applied to Navigation.*

I think, 'Of course, in England, these children would have the advantage of all those ships.'

But in my dream, I take out a volume from a shelf of Lawrence novels. I open it; disappointed, I say, 'But his psychology is nonsense.'

I envied these women who have written memoirs of D. H.

Lawrence, feeling that they had found him some sort of guide or master. I envied Bryher her hero-worship of the psychoanalyst Dr. Hanns Sachs. I cannot be disappointed in Sigmund Freud, only I have this constant obsession that the analysis will be broken by death. I cannot discuss this with the Professor. When he first greeted me, he reminded me of Lawrence.

The Professor said to me today, when I entered the consulting room, 'I was thinking about what you said, about its not being worthwhile to love an old man of seventy-seven.' I had said no such thing and told him so. He smiled his ironical crooked smile. I said, 'I did not say it was not worthwhile, I said I was *afraid.*'

But he confused me. He said, 'In analysis, the person is dead after the analysis is over.' Which person? He said, 'It would not matter if I were seventy-seven or forty-seven.' I now remember that I will be forty-seven on my next birthday. On my birthday, for that one day, Lawrence would be forty-seven.

The Professor had said, 'In analysis, the person is dead after the analysis is over – as dead as your father.'

I remember Norman Douglas saying, 'Just as we're all getting over this Jesus Christ business, trust another Jew to come along and upset all our calculations.'

For one day in the year, H.D. and D. H. Lawrence were twins. But I had not actually realized this until after his death. He was born September 11, 1885: I was born September 10, 1886.

Stephen Guest brought me a copy of *The Man Who Died.* He said, 'Did you know that you are the priestess of Isis in this book?'

Perhaps I would never have read the book if Stephen had not brought it to me. Actually, I might have had at first a slight feeling of annoyance. I had told friends of a book that I wanted to write, actually did write. I called it *Pilate's Wife*. It is the story of the wounded but living Christ, waking up in the rock-tomb. I was certain that my friends had told Lawrence that I was at work on this theme. My first sudden reaction was, 'Now he has taken my story.'

It was not my story. George Moore, among others, had already written it. There is the old myth or tradition that Christ did not die on the Cross.

MARCH 8, 3:15 P.M.

My first week with the Professor began on Wednesday, March 1, a Holy Day, Ash Wednesday, March 1933.

Bryher has arranged for three months, twelve weeks. So, measured by the clock dial, I have moved from the XII to the I. Or I should say, I suppose, counting the hours rather than the minutes, that I have moved from I to II. This is my second week with Sigmund Freud.

I concentrate on the minutes, the minutiae of these hours.

This is March, astrologically the House of Sorrow. It is traditionally the House of the Crucifixion. The astrological months however are not divided exactly as the calendar months. The last week roughly of each calendar month overlaps or begins the new astrological month. So the end of March sometimes coincides with the spiritual vernal equinox, the resurrection.

My father studied or observed the variable orbit of the track of the earth round the sun, variation of latitude, he called it. He spent thirty years on this problem, adding a graph on a map started by Ptolemy in Egypt. The Professor continues a graph started by the ancestors of Ptolemy.

Some call this house, *Pisces* or the *Fishes*, the House of Secret Enemies, but I have seen reference to it as the House of Mysteries.

But we must not talk astrology. In that, at least, my father and Sigmund Freud agree. Nevertheless, in spite of them, or to spite them, I find enchanting parallels in the Ram, the Bull, the Heavenly Twins. We have Yofi, *Leo* certainly.

We have other minutiae, the images on his table, Osiris the sun in his twelve manifestations, as he journeys through the sky, as well as the bronze Isis that he showed me – his companion.

Those two were twins in the old fairy story.

My findings are important to me and have an atmosphere.

Before I could walk properly, I could tell time. Long before I learned my alphabet, I knew the three clock letters.

I would be sent out by my nurse to find out what time it was. There was the grandfather clock on the landing. But surely I could walk there? Perhaps it was easier or pleasanter to slide down the shallow steps, for I always seem to be looking up from the floor at the clock-face. Yes, I could walk. I returned to the nursery with my findings. 'The little hand is at the V.' I could not remember both hands at the same time or else I wanted fresh adventure. The big hand would keep me busy. 'It is at the I, it is at the II,' or much later, 'It has nearly got to the X.'

So I am back again in the mysteries; the childhood of the individual is the childhood of the race, wrote our Professor.

6

MY HALF-BROTHER ERIC and my father talked of time in different dimensions, mean-time or siderial-time (whatever that was) and some other time whose name I can't remember. My interest in 'numbers' was checked at the time of my father's accident and though I did not remember the accident, I remembered how long-division had blocked me or set a wall between my happy and most unhappy school-days. It is significant that my half-brother came to live with us, about this time. He was known generally as the 'young Professor.' It was Eric who finally nursed me over my 'resistance' to long-division. He brought me a copy of *Jane Eyre* and a *Little Women* with the original illustrations. The Little Women wore the bell-skirts that so fascinated me in the old pictures of the Seminary.

I do not know where or how I actually made this transference. But today's transference or yesterday's is explicit in the little green phial of smelling-salts that I carry in my handbag and that I 'accidentally' let fall on the Professor's carpet or left under the pillow of the couch. I do not ask the Professor where he found the little bottle. His air is mock-triumphant as he returns it to me, 'Ah – you forgot this.' He knows that I know the symbolism of the 'lost' umbrella.

And now that this transference is understood between us, I go on to talk of Lawrence. The Professor said that Lawrence had impressed him in the ending of one book. I did not ask him which book. The Professor said that Lawrence impressed him as 'being unsatisfied but a man of real power.'

Freud says there are always a number of explanations for every finding, two or a multiple. In interpreting my own dreams, he said that I showed much more knowledge of psychoanalysis than he had expected of me. Perhaps he meant me to contradict him when he said that my looking at my watch meant that I was bored and wanted the session to end. I did not think that he meant me to take him *pied de la lettre* when he said that I might be impatient with life, desiring even his death, so as to avoid analysis. Or did he mean me to contradict this? What should I say?

There were those statues in the cottage in Cornwall. There

was a row of them along the mantelpiece of an empty room. The house was only partly furnished. I went there in March 1918. It was D. H. Lawrence who had told me of the old house, it was called Rosigran. Lawrence said it was haunted. Was I afraid of ghosts? I said I had never met one.

Here in the semicircle on the table in the other room, is the same or somewhat the same array of images, Osiris, Isis. Perhaps I am afraid of ghosts. But when the Professor said, 'Perhaps you are not happy,' I had no words with which to explain. It is difficult to explain it to myself or to find words to scribble in my note-book. It is not a question of happiness, in the usual sense of the word. It is happiness of the quest.

I am on the fringes or in the penumbra of the light of my father's science and my mother's art – the psychology or philosophy of Sigmund Freud.

I must find new words as the Professor found or coined new words to explain certain as yet unrecorded states of mind or being.

He is Faust, surely.

We retreat from the so-called sciences and go backward or go forward into alchemy. He said, I was impatient with him. He was turning a heavy seal-ring on his finger.

I said that I could not lose him, I had had his books before I met him and would have them again when I left Vienna. There is a formula for Time that has not yet been computed.

7

MARCH 9

I DREAM of a Cathedral. I walk through *Stephens dom* almost daily and, as well, I had been interested in some pictures of

Chartres that I had seen in one of the café's illustrated papers. Two boys are with me in this dream, the older one was showing me around, I felt the little one was *de trop*. I had for some reason tipped the big one, now I must give something to the little one. This annoyed me. (I had been concerned the day before as to the exact tip to give the two page-boys in the hotel.)

I seem to have lost the big boy, so I regretfully annex the smaller.

My two brothers? Or my father and his attractive older brother? My older brother and my father's older brother were both lost in the wars.

The boys in the dream are not recognizably the hotel page-boys. They are ghosts. They are, that is, 'ghosting' for another or others; when the ghosts take form as brothers or as uncle-father, it will no doubt be seen that they again are ghosting. Or rather if we pursue the dream content, the intermediate ghosts, should they manifest, would be seen to be a step between brothers or uncle-father. We are all haunted houses.

It is really the Cathedral that is all-important. Inside the Cathedral we find regeneration or reintegration. This room is the Cathedral.

The Professor said, 'But you are very clever.' It is not I who am clever. I am only applying certain of his own findings to my personal equation. The house is home, the house is the Cathedral. He said he wanted me to feel at home here.

The house in some indescribable way depends on father-mother. At the point of integration or regeneration, there is no conflict over rival loyalties. The Professor's surroundings and interests seem to derive from my mother rather than from my father, and yet to say the 'transference' is to Freud as mother does not altogether satisfy me. He had said, 'And – I must tell you (you were frank with me and I will be frank with you), I do *not* like to be the mother in transference – it always surprises and shocks me a little. I feel so very masculine.' I asked him if others had what he called this mother-transference on him. He said ironically and I thought a little wistfully, 'O, *very* many.'

But now he said he would show me a little new toy. He is delighted with a Coptic clay figure, sent him by a former student. The little image is startlingly like Yofi. Yofi sits as usual on the floor, emblematic, heraldic. The little clay dog looks like Yofi and I cannot help wondering if the donor of the figure on the shelf opposite the couch had noted the striking resemblance of this Etruscan image, with the pointed beard and the thin etched smile, to our Professor.

Today there are red tulips on the famous table with the row or semicircle, Osiris, Isis, Athené, and the others, with the ivory Vishnu in the center.

The Professor has gone into the other room to find another dog to show me. He brings back a broken wooden dog. It is a toy from a tomb in Egypt.

I tell him the only Egyptian dog I remember is one in the Louvre; was the jackal on the standard a dog? The only Egyptian dog that I remember was exactly like his daughter Anna's Wulf.

Yes (I repeated), the Cathedral of my dream was Sigmund Freud. 'No,' he said, 'not me – but analysis.'

It is, as he had said of my grandfather, 'an atmosphere. . . .' The gnomes or gargoyles, the Gothic dragons, bird, beast, and fish of the inner and outer motives, the images of saints and heroes all find their replicas or their 'ghosts' in this room or in these two rooms.

MARCH 10

I had spoken of my disappointment in Havelock Ellis. He had

not been interested in my experience in the Scilly Isles when Bryher took me there, July 1919. It had really been a great shock to me as I had visualized Dr. Ellis, during the time of writing my *Notes on Thought and Vision,* as a saint as well as a savant. The Professor said he had always wondered why a man so situated and not dependent on outside criticism should spend his enormous energy on a superficial documentation of sex. Now the Professor said he felt from my reactions that his own opinion was not unjustified. He said he had been puzzled. 'He records so many funny things that people do but never seems to want to know *why* they do them. You see I *lose* him a little, but I always thought there was something immature about his *Psychology of Sex.*'

I had a dream about my little bottle of smelling-salts, the tell-tale transference symbol. In my dream, I am *salting* my typewriter. So I presume I would salt my savorless writing with the salt of the earth, Sigmund Freud's least utterance.

I have tried to write the story or the novel of my war experience, my first, still-born child and the second, born so fortunately with *Leo* rising in the vernal equinox, *Aries* or the Ram. I have rewritten this story and others that 'ghosted' for it, as in the case of *Pilate's Wife* and *Hedylus,* both historical or classic reconstructions. *Hedylus* had the usual *succès d'estime* that had followed the publication of *Heliodora,* a short volume of poetry, and *Palimpsest,* a rather loosely written long-short-story volume. I feel, too, that the latest volume, *Red Roses for Bronze,* is not altogether satisfactory. I have never been completely satisfied with any of my books, published or unpublished.

Little things, seemingly unimportant, take precedence. I remember how the Professor said that you never know until the analysis is over what is important and what is unimportant. With my memories of Chartres, I recall an illustration in the same paper of a child at a birthday party. It was not an attractive picture, the child was devouring a cream-cake with the cream oozing out onto its frock or pinafore. But children don't wear pinafores nowadays, do they? Birthday memories come back.

My books are not so much still-born as born from the detached intellect. Someone spoke of *Hedylus* as being 'hallucinated writing.'

Yet if I become more 'human' I seem to lose my sense of direction, or my prose style. The poetry is another matter. Yes, the poems are satisfactory but unlike most poets of my acquaintance (and I have known many) I am no longer interested in a poem once it is written, projected, or materialized. There is a feeling that it is only a *part* of myself there.

Perhaps this is partly due to the fact that I lost the early companions of my first writing-period in London, you might say of my 'success,' small and rather specialized as it was. I was rather annoyed with the Professor in one of his volumes. He said (as I remember) that women did not creatively amount to anything or amount to much, unless they had a male counterpart or a male companion from whom they drew their inspiration. Perhaps he is right and my dream of 'salting' my typewriter with the tell-tale transference symbol is further proof of his infallibility.

There were the two chief companions, as there were in the Cathedral dream. Richard Aldington and D. H. Lawrence had both seemed to like my writing. But I was unhappily separated from Aldington and it was impossible at that time to continue my friendship with Lawrence.

But Lawrence returns after his death, though I have not had the courage or the strength to realize this fully.

Lawrence came back with *The Man Who Died*. Whether or not he meant me as the priestess of Isis in that book does not alter the fact that his last book reconciled me to him. Isis is incomplete without Osiris, Judy is meaningless without Punch.

I am certain that I never mentioned Lawrence in my three months' preliminary work with Mary Chadwick at Tavistock Square, in Bloomsbury. I felt that Miss Chadwick could not follow the workings of my creative mind. Talking this over with Dr. Hanns Sachs in Berlin, winter 1931, he agreed that it would be better to continue the work, if possible with a man and preferably one superior to myself. 'The Professor?' he asked me. Of course, I would work with the Professor if he would take me.

Curiously in fantasy I think of a tiger. Myself as a tiger? This tiger may pounce out. Suppose it should attack the frail and delicate old Professor? Do I fear my own terrors of the present situation, the lurking 'beast' may or might destroy him? I mention this tiger as a past nursery fantasy. Suppose it should actually materialize? The Professor says, 'I have my protector.'

He indicates Yofi, the little lioness curled at his feet.

Protector?

I remember the mob scene outside Buckingham Palace, August 4, 1914.

MARCH 11, 9:10 A.M.

I had a dream of an old mirror. The original was set in velvet; sprays of goldenrod were painted on it. I had particularly admired this early creation of my mother's, but the mirror had been banished from downstairs when we moved from Bethlehem, and hung in a small room upstairs at the Flower Observatory house outside Philadelphia. In my dream the long-vanished mirror reappears in our flat at Riant Château, Territet, where my mother had stayed with us in the twenties.

I am very happy with this mirror and touched that my mother should have brought it with her from America.

I re-examine the mirror; there are other flowers but I can only recall the narcissus, some association possibly with the myth of Narcissus falling in love with his reflection in a pool.

Perhaps the books I last wrote of were too self-centered or 'narcissistic' to satisfy my heart. I want a fusion or a transfusion of my mother's art. Though she discarded the velvet with the realistic sprays of goldenrod and other treasures of the same period, there is nothing of da Vinci's nor of Dürer's that can now fire my very entrails with adoration as did those apple-blossoms, daisies, hare-bells, wild roses on her set of 'wedding plates.' It is true, there was a bowl that she brought back from Dresden, from her honeymoon, painted with tulips and other flowers, that I admired almost as much.

Here is the catch. It is easy enough to discard out-moded fashions. The critical faculty can guide and direct us but it is not easy to be critical and at the same time recapture the flame that glowed with unreserved abandon.

The glow returns in the dream. I am happy reviewing my dream and making these notes of them. To continue this last dream, Frances Josepha appears; she with her mother sailed with me in the summer of 1911, on my (and their) first trip to Europe. She was a few years older and we were at that time taken for sisters. Frances found new friends and circumstances separated us. She came in my dream and said, 'Do you remember . . . so-and-so . . . and so-and-so . . . ?' – as if to hurt or humiliate me. I say, 'Nothing I remember matters now except in relation to my telling it or not telling it to Freud.' In my dreams, it seems to me that there is no argument or counter-argument to spoil my delight in this word *Freud*. The Professor has himself pointed out the correspondence of his name Freud with the German *Freude* or joy.

I had known Ezra Pound in America at the same time; now Ezra comes as if to join forces with Frances. He says ironically, 'Since when have you been so happy as this – since yesterday?'

They seemed banded against me; so many people had tried to break my faith. I said to Ezra, 'I couldn't believe Freud would take me – and I am going now every day.' Bryher seems to appear, as she did in actual life, to take the place of Frances. We discuss someone – who? Perhaps it was Ezra or it may possibly have been Lawrence, whose fiery diatribes sometimes reminded me of the early Ezra. In my dream, the Professor restores my faith. 'If I had known Ezra, I could have made him all right,' he says.

In my dream I suddenly associate the Professor's semicircle of little images with bottles. I remembered how, when he returned my smelling-salts, he said that he believed 'this belongs to you – a little *green* bottle?'

When I told the Professor that I had been infatuated with Frances Josepha and might have been happy with her, he said, 'No – biologically, no.' For some reason, though I had been so happy with the Professor (Freud – *Freude*), my head hurt and I felt unnerved. Perhaps it was because at the end I tried to tell him of one special air-raid when the windows of our room in Mecklenburgh Square were shattered.

8

6:30

THE PROFESSOR had said, when I told him of Frances and Ezra and their apparent lack of sympathy or understanding of my delight in the analysis, that I was escaping from unwonted memories or putting them aside; he said I was leaving the situation or the solution to psychoanalysis.

For the time being, I leave my conflicts, trusting they will be solved or resolved in the dream.

In the dream we wander along the Nile in Egypt or the Lehigh or the Delaware Rivers in Pennsylvania, or we find some portion of the 'lost' home or the 'lost' love by the Danube, the Thames, or Tiber. The dream in that sense is itself Osiris, the world beyond, death or the world across the threshold of waking life, sleep. We do not always know when we are dreaming.

I tried to outline several experiences I had had on my first trip to Greece. I have tried to write of these experiences. I fact, it is the fear of losing them, forgetting them, or just giving them up as neurotic fantasies, residue of the war, confinement and the epidemic, that drives me on to begin again and again a fresh outline of the 'novel.' It is obviously Penelope's web that I am weaving.

I can decide that my experiences were the logical outcome of illness, separation from my husband, and loss of the friendship of Lawrence; but even so I have no technique with which to deal with the vision. It was as if a curtain had dropped, what Stephen Guest once referred to as an 'asbestos curtain' between the ten years of my life away from America, and the then (spring 1920) present. I had sailed from New York, as I remember in summer 1911, but I believe I met Frances the year before, 1910, the comet-year.

The first decade of my adventure opened with the Argo, *Floride*, a small French-line steamer, sailing for Havre. The second decade of my adventure with the Argo, *Borodino*, a boat belonging to 'one of the lines,' Bryher's phrase for her father's shipping. The third decade of my cruise or quest may be said to have begun in London with my decision to undertake a serious course of psychoanalysis, for my own immediate benefit and also to fortify me for the future.

We cruised about my childhood. Miss Chadwick was most helpful. She could not follow the later developments. We cruised back and forth, Switzerland and a short visit to Berlin. Dr. Sachs was going on to see his family in Vienna so I preceded him there, via Prague. I had only a few talks with Dr. Sachs in Vienna, but it was there I decided that the best thing, if possible, was to work direct with the Professor. Sorting books, manuscripts, note-books, I felt as if I were indeed making ready for a last voyage out. But in the general house-cleaning, I did not get on any further with the 'novel,' though I could not bring myself to destroy the last rough copies. There it is hanging over me, that 'novel.' The man on the *Borodino*, a certain Mr. Van Eck (we will call him for convenience) was a man on the *Borodino*, but the Man was not Mr. Van Eck.

I did not encounter him often. We were three weeks at sea, that is counting time put in at Malta and Gibraltar. There was a terrific storm, there had been nearly a gale crossing the Atlantic that first time, but it amounted to more than a gale if you take into consideration the size and condition of the *Floride*, then on its last crossing. The *Borodino* was more than seaworthy, it was metal-lined, had been used as a mailship in the navy during the war. It had been selected for us for this reason by Bryher's father. There were still floating mines everywhere.

I tell the Professor in detail of how I met the Man who was not Mr. Van Eck. It is true I thought he was Mr. Van Eck but there was a catch. I knew that from the beginning. Mr. Van Eck had a startling heavy scar above his left eyebrow; it was noted in his passport, under any noticeable marks. The captain I remember spoke of it. The Man on the boat had no scar above his left eyebrow.

So far, so good.

I have written or so often tried to write of my experience of the Man on the boat that it is not difficult to tell the story to the Professor. The chief 'meeting' was in February, a few days out from the port of London. There had been rough weather and I was told that the Bay (I had not heard the Bay of Biscay referred to as the Bay before) was always rough, anyway. I had been trudging round the deck with Bryher and Dr. Ellis, who was with us. I wore an old blue jacket, a beret as they now call our old tam-o'-shanter, and low deck-shoes. The costume is homely but suitable to the occasion and as I slip and slide on my unusually sea-worthy legs, I am indeed in a new element. I am in an old element too; I am adolescent and a fresh strength has come to me even in these few days at sea, out from London.

I could not have invented a costume that would have been more suitable, that would better have expressed my state of renewed girlhood or youth. I was surprised that the deck was completely deserted and that the wind had fallen. It was, by clock time, before dinner as I had gone to the stateroom to change as usual. Perhaps in the stateroom I had thrown myself down on my bunk to rest for a few minutes before undertaking the arduous task of unearthing fresh clothes from the suitcase. It was a small cabin but the best on the boat. But the boat was not officially a traveling vessel. There had been double rows of partitioned bunks run up, one imagined, for convenience of the few travelers taken on as a special privilege (at that time, sailing accommodations had to be booked months or even years in advance). There was, as I remember, perhaps one hook on the door. In any case, it was very rough. Perhaps I had thrown myself down on the bunk for a few minutes' rest before changing.

Perhaps I was there in the bunk, normally resting, when I climbed the now level flight of steps to the upper deck. Well, it was quiet. But the fresh air was stimulating, a fresh tang, a fresh taste though it had all been a sort of breath of resurrection anyway, since we sailed down the river on that late afternoon of early February 1920.

Still the deck was, considering all things, in some special way swept you might say and garnished. There were no odd deck chairs about, no boy stooping to rescue cushions or assemble forgotten rugs. To be sure, there had not been many people on deck when we had parted with Dr. Ellis, that few minutes ago.

Perhaps it was more than a few minutes, but we were crossing something, 'the line'? What line? We were coasting along in the Bay, along the shore of Europe, but Europe was out of sight, to one's left as one faced the prow. I had laughed at Dr. Ellis with his inherited ship-captain language, starboard, larboard, though as a school-girl I had been meticulous enough myself and knew my port and starboard, hard alee and all the rest. All that had left me. I was satisfied with right and left, front and back. 'Shall we go forward?' Bryher would say. Well – shall we go forward?

The wind must have fallen very suddenly. Perhaps too, here nearing Portugal, the night would come with that un-Nordic balm and suavity that I sometimes missed in the close sky of winter England. Anyway, there was a violet light over the sea.

I must get Bryher, I thought; Bryher must not miss this, but as I am about to turn back I see Mr. Van Eck standing by the deck rail, to my *right*, as I stand there at the head of the ship stairs.

Well – he sees me. I must at least say good-evening. I notice to my surprise that he is somewhat taller than myself. I had not thought he was quite so tall, though he stood a good military height, with broad shoulders, rather square in build though not over-heavy. He is taller than I thought him. I must not stare at Mr. Van Eck. I am always afraid he will catch my eyes focused, in some sort of uncontrollable fascination, on that curious deep scar over his left eyebrow. All the same, one cannot in decency *not* meet the eyes of the person one is greeting. His eyes are uncovered; Mr. Van Eck wore thick-rimmed glasses.

His eyes are more blue than I had thought, it is mist-blue, sea-blue.

His hair at his temples is not so thin as I had imagined. Mr. Van Eck had told me he was forty-four or would be on the 10th of March. I am September 10, so we were, as the astrological charts show, not in opposition, the *Fishes* being opposite *Virgo*. But we are in the straight line of affinity. I did not tell him the date of my birthday, but I worked it out; I was thirty-three, and when Peter Van Eck was forty-four in March, I would still be thirty-three until the following September.

He is taller. He is older – no, he must be younger. It is near evening, it is this strange light. But the light is not strange.

One cannot stare. But it is certain the scar is not there.

On his right as he stands now facing me, there is the coast of Europe – Portugal? On his right as he stands there, there is an indented coastline. 'Land,' I said. I did not in my thought realize that land, were there land, would be on the other side of the boat. Or had the boat turned round? Or were these some off-lying islands of which I in my ignorance knew nothing? There were dolphins.

Yes, there were dolphins. But there had been talk of dolphins, sea-pigs someone called them, perhaps the engineer on his way to Euboea, who sat next to Dr. Ellis at table. The four of us sat, right, left: Bryher and myself were next to the captain at the one long table. Next to Bryher was Dr. Ellis; to my left at table was Mr. Van Eck.

The dolphins are joined by other dolphins; they make a curiously unconvincing pattern, leaping in rhythmic order like crescent moons or half-moons out of the water, a flight or a dance of dolphins. Yet, they are dolphins. Didn't the engineer on the way to Euboea say he had been looking for a sea-pig?

We are in March, *Pisces*, the *Fishes*, but I don't think I thought that.

I don't know what I thought. I thought, Mr. Van Eck for some reason (perhaps he is a secret agent) 'makes up.' Could he rub in or put on that scar? Well, perhaps it wasn't Mr. Van Eck who 'made up' as a secret agent; perhaps the secret agent made up as Mr. Van Eck.

No, I did not know this, think all of this out, at that exact moment, in February. Yes, it was February. It was not yet March; February is *Aquarius*, the house of friends. . . .

MARCH 13

The Professor said he was curious to see how the story would proceed, now we had the frame.

I too was curious. If the Professor could not solve my problem, no one could. I told him how the first evening out I was very upset as I had on my left a deaf old Canadian lady who was on her way to Athens to visit a niece who had married a Greek lawyer. I am particularly unhappy when I have to raise my voice in speaking and I visualized having to carry on polite table talk in this strained and unnatural manner, the whole voyage out. Even so, it would not have mattered so much if the whole table had not appeared to stop their buzz of conversation every time I lifted my voice to make some inane remark or in politeness tried my best to answer noncommittally when the old lady asked me about my plans and why was I on this boat and how had I managed to get on it?

I had not then distinguished the Alexandrian family, or I did not know that they were on the way to Alexandria – 'Alex' the big boy called it. It was 'Alex' and 'Gib' too, with the engineer and a missionary (I later gathered) who sat within, as it were, hailing distance. But neither the missionary nor the Alexandrian tobacco merchant (as I afterwards found he was) nor the engineer bound for Euboea helped me in the least in my predicament.

It seemed a miracle, after two nights in this anguish, to find I had another companion.

It was Mr. Van Eck. I don't know how he got there. The old lady, it is true, had retired to her cabin for the rest of the trip. I suppose seasoned travelers, as all these seemed to be, know how to arrange these things. To me it was little less than a miracle to find, the third day, instead of the deaf old lady, a sympathetic, slightly middle-aged man-of-the-world, easy and affable, making witty remarks *sotto voce* about our fellow passengers.

I was fascinated with Peter Van Eck. He had traveled widely, had lived in Greece for some time, had worked on excavations in Crete, was an architect by profession and he said an artist by choice but he had had little choice in the matter. He had been in Egypt at one time, helping to restore some Caliph's or Khedive's shrine or tomb. These words were new to me. He said something was 'Khedival' to Bryher across the table; I don't remember what. I only remember hearing the word for the first time.

But I had my reservations. An asbestos curtain had dropped between me and my past, my not-so-far-past bitter severance from love and friendship.

I repeated, 'We were three weeks on the way.' The Professor said, 'So-o slow?'

We ran away from Dr. Ellis at Algeciras and went with Mr. Van Eck for a walk through a cork forest; the ground was starry with February narcissus. This was Mr. Van Eck, it was not the Man on the boat, but I had then neither the wit, the temerity, nor the courage to work this all out. If Mr. Van Eck was the Man on the boat, then I lost something. If Mr. Van Eck was not the Man on the boat, then I lost something. I don't know why, but at Malta I told Bryher that I did not want the four of us to drive out to the old town as Mr. Van Eck suggested. I think I wanted to be alone with Bryher, to think out something that I did not question, or that I did not put into a question. To answer the question meant loss of one or the other, Mr. Van Eck or the Man on the boat.

Sometimes Mr. Van Eck was the Man on the boat but he was not the Man on the boat that I met the first time in the Bay. I should have known. I did know, though I could not yet admit it, that not only were the dolphins unconvincing but the sea itself was impossible. That is, it was all right at the time but you do not have a quiet sea and a boat moving with no tremor, with no quiver or pulse of engine, on a sea that is level yet broken in a thousand perfectly peaked wavelets like the waves in the background of a Botticelli. No, it was all wrong.

Yet it was so supremely natural that I turned to Mr. Van Eck, at the table. 'It was beautiful watching the dolphins,' I said. 'If only Bryher had been with us.' Bryher said, I thought a little sullenly, 'Where were you anyway?' I said, 'I was on deck. I dashed up for a breath of air and to see the sunset. I was on deck watching the dolphins with Mr. Van Eck.' I turned to Mr. Van Eck for confirmation.

He smiled at Bryher across the table. He had an engaging manner. The captain said, 'Dolphins? The wireless-operator is our dolphin expert. He reported no dolphins.' 'But there were dolphins.' I turned to Mr. Van Eck again for confirmation. 'Which way were they swimming?' said the captain. I indicated above the table the direction of the frieze of flying dolphins. 'They were swimming *this* way,' I said, indicating a line 'forward,' past Mr. Van Eck down the table. 'That's right,' said the captain, 'that's how they would be swimming. They swim with the wind. I must ask the wireless-operator.'

But now I said to the Professor, 'Where was I, if Bryher couldn't find me?'

Perhaps this is an old conundrum. Perhaps there is no answer to it or it may be dangerous to ask it, for the wrong answer (as with the Sphinx in Egypt) may bring death. At least, I could record the details of my experience, could note them down, could weave and re-weave the threads, the tapestry on this frame. It did not really matter where I was. Perhaps it was a story like the erlking. Perhaps, as is more likely, it was a story like Algernon Blackwood's *Centaur*.

I had read *The Centaur* a number of times, first in America. There was that same theme, that same absolute and exact minute when everything changed on a small passenger boat (as I remember) on the way to Greece. At an exact moment, the boat slipped into enchantment. So here, at an exact moment, by clock time, on an exact map, on the way to the Pillars of Hercules, on a boat that was bound for the port of Athens, there was a 'crossing the line.' I think in *The Centaur*, the narrator or hero knew the minute, the second that the line was crossed. I, the narrator of this story, did not know I had crossed the line.

When I did realize it, it was too late, I could not approach Mr. Van Eck. He was on his way to Delhi.

Delhi, Delphi?

They arrange things that way, I suppose. If I had realized the story at the time of our parting in Athens, perhaps there would have been no parting. In which case, I would have lost the story.

At that table in the long salon, names were batted about to and fro, up and down, like old-fashioned table-tennis balls. London, Gibraltar, Algeciras, Malta, Athens, Delhi, Alexandria, Cairo. . . . I said to Mr. Van Eck that last morning at breakfast, 'I suppose I'll run across you in one of the capitals of Europe.' I did not want to make any definite arrangement for meeting him in Athens. 'I'll meet *you* in the Propylae,' he said.

Bryher and I met him in the Propylae with Dr. Ellis. But he let us go on alone through the gates, to the Parthenon.

8 P.M.

I feel limp and frustrated. I was annoyed at the end of my session as Yofi would wander about and I felt that the Professor was more interested in Yofi than he was in my story. I was annoyed because I heard someone laughing outside the door. I seldom hear or register what is going on in the waiting room or the hall. The Professor said, 'So the memories are faded?' Perhaps he felt that I was really trying too hard to make a dramatic sequence of this story that was all 'an atmosphere. . . .'

I snapped at him rather, 'No – *not* faded.'

The Professor asked me if I had seen this man again. I said, 'Twice in London.' Perhaps the tone of my voice conveyed to him what I felt. Mr. Van Eck in London was not the Man on the boat.

MARCH 14, 2:40 P.M.

A familiar nightmare last night. I was in one hotel or pension, Bryher and my mother were in another. I return to my room to find an irate landlady has removed all my clothes and belongings to another room, without consulting me. I am annoyed but in my dream too frightened to be other than polite. There are several children playing about. The children are indifferent but apparently not inimical. The landlady glares at me, 'But we have *no* room here; you must get right out.'

I manage somehow to get my clothes, I am overburdened with them and with a number of awkward packages but I manage finally to reach Bryher and my mother. We are in Florence along the Arno but the Arno is only a riverbed with a few footprints. My mother says, 'You are only safe on *this* side of the river.'

I am still overburdened and lost. My mother died just six years ago, in March. We had stayed in a hotel in Florence, Lungarno, along the Arno. I had first visited Florence in 1912 with both my parents. At this time too, fourteen years ago, I was waiting for the arrival of my child. I had been taken with what the Professor called the epidemic, in a pension in Ealing waiting to go into Saint Faith's Nursing Home. There had been death in the house. Afterwards, I learned how shocked Bryher had been when she came to see me. The landlady had said, 'But who is to see to the funeral if she dies?'

The dream content is commonplace. But I wake with heartache – heartache, yes, in the conventional romantic sense, and heartache or actual physical pain that frightens me.

I recover over my breakfast tray, Vienna coffee and rolls, and I go out and get the Sigmund Freud engraving that I had ordered a few days ago in the shop on the Ringstrasse.

9

7 P.M.

I TOLD THE Professor of the shock after my nightmare, as of a blow on my heart. He asked first of Van Eck – was it an Austrian name? He said, 'I have an idea.' He rushed off and brought back a leather case, and showed me the name, stamped inside the folder. It was *Vaneck*.

He was interested to hear that Mr. Van Eck was the

adopted son of the Victorian painter. He asked of the nationality. I explained that I thought it was a *nom-de-guerre;* they were a Dutch family, settled in London. I said painting reminded me of my mother. I told him how as children we had admired her painting and boasted to visitors, 'My mother *painted* that.' My mother was morbidly self-effacing.

I went on to say how difficult it had been to reassemble the story of Peter Van Eck, when after all it was a conventional meeting or voyage-out romance. The Professor asked me to interpret my dream of the two rooms in the hotel or pension. I told him I thought it was fear of being moved, at the time of my pregnancy; perhaps it was fear of death. He asked me for more 'historical detail.' I told him of various incidents during the war years when I had stayed in small rooms to be near my husband at his various training units. How difficult it was to get in anywhere at that time and of how once, coming from Buckinghamshire to see the doctor and being caught late in the fog, I had to find a room for the night. Wandering around Bloomsbury, a perfect stranger spoke to me. 'I have a room you can have,' he said. It seemed impossible, but he opened one of those green doors in a row of green doors and introduced me to the landlady. 'This lady is taking my room for the night,' he said. This did happen. Telling it, it seems part of a dream.

The Professor said, 'But I know who the bad landlady is.' I asked innocently, 'Who?' He said, 'Myself.' I repudiated this and then remembered how upset I had been with Mary Chadwick of Tavistock Square, Bloomsbury, when she said at the end of our three months' session, 'You *do* like to talk, don't you?' I told this to the Professor; he said, 'But Miss Chadwick and your work with her is only a forerunner of myself.' I said, 'No. She was a competent nurse, but not a doctor.'

The Professor said, there must be other 'historical data' to do with my fear of being turned out. Yes, there were many actual associations. I remembered once, staying in Rome with my parents, running up to my room after a tired day's excursion and finding the cupboard empty and nothing belonging to me on the dressing table. I had been moved downstairs to another bedroom. It was not the annoyance of not being consulted that so much concerned me as the shock of rushing upstairs and finding my clothes, shoes, and so on had disappeared mysteriously. I tell the Professor that when I go back to my room at the Regina, I seem to brace myself before unlocking the door, lest I find I have been moved out. I am reminded of the hotels we stayed in, in Florence, Rome, and Naples. I feel here that I am in an Italian or near-Italian city.

3:30 P.M.

Now having my early tea, I remember how the Professor asked me why I was so happy to have the hour 5 P.M. for my sessions. I told him how I had associated my happiest memories of early London with the inevitable four o'clock or five o'clock tea and that here I could dream over my note-book, preparing myself for the happiness of talking with him afterwards. He said again that he did not want me to prepare. I could not explain adequately that I did not. He does not, apparently, want me to take notes, but I must do that.

I remember how happy I was with the children across the street, playing at tea parties. We had our intermediate set of dishes for these occasions. My mother got me a set as I was so excited about the Williams' 'real tea set.' It was intermediate between the grown-ups and the dolls.

I think it was my seventh birthday that my mother got me this set. There was a gilt edge to the cups and saucers and the bread-and-butter-sized plates. There were knots of violets.

10

6:40 P.M.

THE PROFESSOR found me reading in the waiting room. He said that I must borrow any books of his that I wanted. We talked again of Yofi. I asked of Yofi's father. Yofi is to be a mother. He told me that Yofi's first husband was a black chow and Yofi had one black baby, 'as black as the devil.' It died when it was three-quarters of a year old. Now the new father is lion-gold and the Professor hopes that Yofi's children will survive, this time. He said, if there are two puppies, the father's people have one, but if only one, 'it stays a Freud.'

The Professor asked me if I had noticed 'trouble in walking.' I did not know what he meant. I said I was feeling well and enjoyed going about. But he said, 'I mean, on the streets.' I did not even then quite realize what he meant; I said that I felt at home here and never frightened. I said, 'The people in the shops are so courteous.' The Professor said, 'Yes . . . to a *lady.*'

The Professor asked me again of 'historical associations' of moving or being moved. I told him of some of my findings.

I said that there were no doubt infantile associations about 'leaving the room' or being sent out of the room because one had been naughty. He said, 'Yes, the infantile memory or association is often unhappy.'

But leaving home was not always an unhappy matter. I was sent to stay with a young childless aunt at one time, and will never forget the giant rag doll, a treasure from her childhood that she gave me to play with. She it was who first gave me little gauze bags of assorted beads and helped me to string them. I had had a dream with Miss Chadwick that my uncle's name was Vaneck; it was really Frederick.

I spoke again of our toy animals and he reminded me of my tiger fantasy. Wasn't there a story, 'the woman and the tiger,' he asked. I remembered 'The Lady or the Tiger.'

Today, I entered my third week.

11

MARCH 16, 7 P.M.

I SAW A volume of Arthur Waley's on the shelf, and asked the Professor if he knew him. He said no. I started to tell the Professor how I had met Waley in London in the very early days, at the British Museum where I was reading and how he asked me to tea in the Museum Tea Room. We discussed an umbrella I was carrying, *en-tout-cas* they had called it, at the shop, to my amusement. Later, during the war, I met Arthur Waley at Iseult Gonne's flat in Chelsea. I said I thought Waley was a Jew, Freud said he thought so, but 'he has tampered with his name.'

I went on to tell Freud why I had kept away from psycho-analysis in London, had read practically nothing until recent years, how Waley in our Buckingham Mansions, Kensington, flat, about 1920, had suggested that a friend of his might help Bryher, how Dr. Ellis discouraged it, but how finally Bryher went for a few sessions to _____.

(At this moment, writing on a marble-topped café table, a tiny bunch of violets is placed on my note-book. I want to cry. In my embarrassment, I only gave thirty groschen; but the beggar with the shoe-box seemed pleased and vanished. In the same way, violets were laid on the pages of a paperbound copy of Euripides' *Ion*, open on the table of my Corfu Hotel Belle Venise bedroom. It seemed a 'mystery' but Bryher must have left them.)

I went on to tell how I parted from Van Eck, in the drawing room of the Hotel Grand Bretagne in Athens. I said I was frozen.

Dr. Ellis, who was with us on the boat but in another hotel in Athens, went back to London after a few weeks. How cold it was – wind from Siberia – there was a stove in the corner of our elegant drawing room, everything was ormolu and gilded mirror frames – no sticks, no coal. Spanish influenza was raging there again.

Freud asked if Bryher had had it. Not dangerously, I explained. One of her father's business associates there suggested that we leave Athens. We went up the Gulf of Corinth on the advice of this Mr. Crowe. In the night we stopped at Itea, below the landing or port for Delphi.

I tell the Professor how happy I was at Corfu – flowers, spring, orange trees, lead-pencil cypresses, Mouse Island or Böcklein's *Toteninsel*. I told him of Bryher's care of me, our walks and drives, and said the friendship seemed to have adjusted me to normal conditions of life. Freud qualified, 'Not normal, so much as ideal.'

He wanted to know of the pictures, that I called Writing on the Wall, but the time was almost up so I simply stated that Van Eck all this time was in my mind. Bryher knew of this. The Professor said the problem was more subtle, more intricate than he had first imagined.

He said he did not wish me to *prepare* for my sessions with him. I said I did not. I spoke of my delight in the idea of resolving old problems.

When I told him of the Scilly Isles experience, the transcendental feeling of the two globes or the two transparent half-globes enclosing me, I said I supposed it was some form of pre-natal fantasy. Freud said, 'Yes, obviously; you have found the answer, good – good.'

MARCH 17, 2:25 P.M.

Had strange dream of huge blackbirds. (Mr. Crowe of yesterday?) They peck or bite at my ankles with their great beaks. I am terrified. In some way, I am rescued by a youth or young man, and the polished black beaks of the birds turn to ebony anklets above my bare feet.

A friend of my school-days comes. She is looking for rooms. *Rooms* again. There is a confused sequence of a house or mansion with many rooms – my father's house? I like Matilda and am glad to see her – but there is the old predicament! Will she interfere with my *room* or *rooms*? Is this a birth-anxiety? Bryher writes of joining me here later, with my daughter.

6:40 P.M.

The Professor asked me to interpret the dream of the blackbirds.

Freud said the man in the dream had given me womanhood, so he charmed the birds.

12

6:40 P.M.

TODAY I TOLD the Professor of the picture-writing, or the Writing on the Wall as I called it. He wanted to know particulars of the exact size of the projected pictures that I saw in the bedroom of the Hotel Belle Venise in Corfu, the actual time it took for the series to materialize, what time of day was it? I looked round the room and found what I was looking for; on one of his Greek vases there was an image of Victory, or the Niké as I called her, of the picture sequence. I said, 'Ah, there she is.'

The Professor and I went over to the glass case. Some of the pictures as I saw and described them might have been Greek vase silhouettes.

7:40 P.M.

I had taken a photograph of Bryher to show the Professor. He said it might have been a page in an Italian fresco.

The Professor said, 'She is *only* a boy.' Then he said, 'It is very clear.' Of another photograph, he said, 'She looks like an Arctic explorer.' He liked another snapshot of my daughter with Bryher on the terrace of the house at La Tour. I told the Professor that they both might be coming later to Vienna. He said, 'I would so like to see them.' This made me very happy.

He said Bryher's letters were 'very kind, very pliable,' though she herself looked in the pictures 'so decisive, so unyielding.' I told him how staunch Bryher had been and loyal, and how she arranged everything on our numerous journeys. When I told him of the Writing on the Wall he asked me if I was frightened. I said I was not, but I was afraid that Bryher was frightened for me. He asked again about the lighting of the room, of possible reflections or shadows. I described the room again, the communicating door, the door out to the hall and the one window. He asked if it was a French window. I said, 'No – one like that,' indicating the one window in his room.

8:10 P.M.

I sit in the Café Victoria, on a cushioned corner-bench, under an immense chandelier. I think of Venice when I look at the reflecting glass crystals.

MARCH 18, 10:40 A.M.

I dream of my young mother. We are on the porch of our first house at Bethlehem. My brother is only a year younger, but I feel immensely superior as I watch him crawl over the floor. He creeps, crawls, or walks very swiftly on all four legs. I think he is very clever, this 'little dog.' I try to indicate this to my mother. She says, 'But he will get his arms dirty and spoil his dress.' The baby dodges into the open hall door. I say to my mother, very wise and tolerant, 'But what does it matter? It is good for him to crawl about, it will make a difference to his whole life, it will strengthen his back, his arms, and legs.' He crawls out of the house again and I stand him on his feet and fling my arms about him in a delirium of devotion.

I connect this dream with the Professor's remark about Bryher, 'She is *only* a boy,' and with the fact that Bryher writes of coming with my child to visit me here in Vienna.

I had a later dream. Bryher's pet name for Dr. Hanns Sachs is 'the turtle.' A friend, an American resident in England, turns up here for some odd reason. The turtle-pond is high up in the hills, Switzerland, no doubt. I myself confront George Plank by this turtle-pond, bearing proudly a *hen's egg*. There is a woman writing. She says, 'You girls – you show off in your Elizabethan doublets.' I have a feeling of vast superiority to George, who is actually an artist and a sympathetic friend. I have a feeling, however, that he would not respond to psycho-analysis, though not inimical as I felt Frances and Ezra to be in the early dream sequence.

4 P.M.
The Professor told me a few days ago that if he lived another fifty years, he would still be fascinated and curious about the vagaries and variations of the human mind or soul.

13

7 P.M.
I WAS FIVE MINUTES LATE as Alice Modern had popped in about 4:30. The Professor met me at once, said my story of the picture-writing or the Writing on the Wall, 'has made me think very hard.'

I asked him about the dogs; both go away over the weekend.

He does not like cats; he finds monkeys are too near. 'We have not the satisfaction of their being like us, nor the satisfaction of their being enemies.'

I told him about the little statues or images in the house that Lawrence had first spoken of in Cornwall. He asked me what the images were? I said that there was a painted Osiris on the shelf; seated at the end was a bronze Isis – there was I thought an egg-shaped mummy-owl.

The Professor said, 'Come and see if we can find them.'

We went into the other room; he brought out various treasures from behind the glass doors. We spoke of a Sekmet that he showed me. I told the Professor of the cat-headed image in the little temple off the great temple of Karnak. He was amused to hear of the iron grille they had had to place at the temple entrance, because of the hysterical moonlight visitors. I said that the Arabs held the image in special awe, they were terrified to this day of the cat- or lion-headed goddess.

We looked over the images in one of the other cases; there was a winged Greek figure – tanagra? The Professor brought out a wooden Osiris (or Osiris-like image) blackened by time or else deliberately painted, as if with a sort of tar or pitch. There was another green-blue stone Osiris. The Professor said, 'They are called the *answerers*, as their doubles or ka-s come when called.'

We went back to the couch.

I told him of the scenes or pictures that I myself had conjured up or acted out for Bryher, one of our last evenings in the Belle Venise. Bryher had seemed unhappy or remote; her mood frightened and saddened me. To amuse her, really, I began to act out what I called Indian dance-pictures. There was a girl in the mountains, there was a medicine man seeking for plants in the woods, there was another laughing, singing – our old friend Minnehaha; there were others as well: a Spanish woman, South-Sea Islanders, a Japanese girl, and a young priest from Tibet. The Professor said, 'It was a poem-series the acting was drama, half-motivated by desire to comfort Bryher and neither 'delirium' nor 'magic.' I had suggested that this might be some form of possession.

The Professor repeated, 'You see, after all, you are a poet.' He dismissed my suggestion of some connection with the old mysteries, magic or second-sight. But he came back to the Writing on the Wall. The drama, as he called it, he said held no secret from him; but the projected pictures, seen in daylight, puzzled him.

He went on with it, could I now with my eyes closed still see the pictures? I said, 'Yes, and with my eyes open.' He said this was possibly a 'symptom of importance.' I said that I wished I had asked an artist friend to sketch the series for me, so that I could have shown it to him direct. He said that would have been no use. "There would be value in the pictures only if you yourself drew them.'

9:10

We talked a little of ghosts. I wanted to tell him of the many curious legends of Cornwall and of how I myself had heard the famous 'knockers' when I was there in 1918. They were believed by the inhabitants to come out of the disused mine-shafts. They are the exact counterpart, though I did not have time to speak of this, of the gnomes or dwarfs of the old German legends. The 'knockers,' however, were not ghostly presences, they knocked forcibly, almost violently, and often.

I did tell the Professor of a great-grandmother who heard her son calling to her. She ran out in the garden to meet him (in Pennsylvania). Her son was in the West Indies. It was some time after that news reached them that her son had died at the exact moment she had rushed into the garden to welcome him home.

MARCH 20, MONDAY

I spent a happy Sunday at the galleries; I found Tiziano Vec., Jacopa da Strada, 1477–1576, and Palma Gioime, 1544–1628, with statues . . . and Giov. Batt. Moroni, 1520–1578. One of the paintings of a fine, intellectually weathered renaissance Italian, standing by a table, with small statues, suggested to me the portrait of Sigmund Freud with his row of little images before him on the table.

14

6:40 P.M.

I WENT UP TO Mrs. Burlingham's apartment at 4:20. She was quiet, slim, and pretty in her art-craft simple consulting room or sitting room that Freud's architect son had decorated for her. Like the Professor, she had a few Greek treasures. Her little grey Bedlingham scurried under the couch but crawled out later to make friends with me. I met her daughter, my own child's age, and a boy of seventeen. Another child was having a music lesson in the next room. I was a little disconcerted by Mrs. Burlingham's reserved, shy manner, and her reminding me that I was due at five, downstairs with the Professor.

Then down to Freud. . . . I told him of the visit. Then I felt a little lost. Perhaps that was partly because of the dream I had last had. I tried desperately to get back to my flat in Sloane Street, London. The flat is at the top of the house. As I enter the downstairs hall, a man and then a rough boy barred my way to the staircase and seemed to threaten me. I did not dare challenge them. . . . (I could not tell the Professor that this terror was associated in my mind with news of fresh Nazi atrocities.) As I stood threatened and terrified I call, loudly,

'Mother.' I am out on the pavement now. I look up at the window of my flat. It has different curtains or a suggestion of Venetian blinds. A figure is standing there, holding a lighted candle. It is my mother.

I was overpowered with happiness and all trace of terror vanished.

8:20 P.M.

We talked of Crete. I told him how disappointed I was on the cruise last spring. It was too rough to land. There were dolphins playing about the boat, anchored off the rocky shore; there was a permanent rainbow from the sea spray. We saw the chapel high on the slopes where it was reputed Zeus had been born, or nursed. We spoke of Sir Arthur Evans and his work there. The Professor said that we two met in our love of antiquity. He said his little statues and images helped stabilize the evanescent idea, or keep it from escaping altogether. I asked if he had a Cretan serpent-goddess. He said, 'No.' I said that I had known people in London who had had some connection with Crete at one time, and that I might move heaven and earth, and get him a serpent-goddess. He said, 'I doubt if even *you* could do that.'

The Professor speaks of the mother-layer of fixation being the same in girls and boys, but the girl usually transfers her affection or (if it happens) her fixation to her father. Not always. The Crete mother-goddess is associated with the boy or youth in the wall-painting of the crocus fields. We talk of Aegina too. The Professor went on about the growth of psychoanalysis and how mistakes were made in the beginning, as it was not sufficiently understood that the girl did not invariably transfer her emotions to her father.

He asked, 'Was your father a little cold, a little stiff?' I explained again that he was what is known as 'typically New

England,' though he was one remove from New England, his father having moved to the west. The Professor said he thought my dance-dramas at Corfu were really a sort of display or entertainment for my *mother*. Did your mother sing to you? I said she had a resonant beautiful voice but that she had some sort of block or repression about singing. Our grandmother loved me to sing to her, old-fashioned hymns for the most part. My older brother and I sang little nursery songs to our mother's accompaniment. The Professor said this held together. 'It will simplify out, even more.' I told him again that my mother died in spring, at this very time, and again I remember that Lawrence died too, in March.

15

MARCH 21, TUESDAY

THE BEAUTIFUL ENGRAVING that I have of the Professor is propped up on my dressing table. It becomes the 'answerer,' like the particular Osiris-image that he showed me.

6:30 P.M.

The Professor was touched with Bryher's note and her gift to the Society. We talked of the political situation.

There are no frontiers of the spirit.

Yet I am torn by intense emotions of antipathy.

Last night, I had my old train-nightmare. I am going somewhere vaguely undefined with my daughter and Alice, who was at one time her governess. A uniformed official searches our bags. He finds my traveling-flask. Cognac? I attempt no explanation nor apology. The official ('censor,' the Professor?) finds another bottle hidden under the seat. There are more bottles. He collects the lot in an empty suitcase and orders us to follow him.

My daughter and Alice and I are lost somewhere, on some dangerous way, *down* some steps.

The Professor asked me my association; I said I had no precise association, I was just afraid of being found out. He said, 'Maybe, some scruple.' Conscience?

There are so many associations with trains. I recall one in particular when I arrived on the boat train, just after dawn in Paris. My French coffee and rolls at the station buffet were indescribably *France*. Again, I had got away. Loving England, there was yet, always, that almost hysterical sense of escape, once across the channel. I could even recall the wall-paintings of the Gare–du Nord? Normandy with apple trees, a sea wall and blue sky broken by a foreground of – olives? orange trees? While I was having my coffee in the almost empty buffet, a boy arrived with a huge market basket piled with roses. The manager or waiter selected a handful of roses and laid them by my plate.

Then I remember an incident that preceded the train dream. I am being fitted for a green gown. I stand before a mirror and extend my foot. I wear a beautifully cut classic, yet suitably modern, Greek sandal.

The Professor said, 'You tell it so beautifully.'

Before I leave, I fold the silver-grey rug. I have been caterpillar, worm, snug in the chrysalis.

The Professor touches the little bell to warn the maid that this last analysand is about to leave. His elbow concludes its bird-wing dismissing gesture. The Professor says, 'We have gone into deep matters.'

They called my father the Professor and my half-brother the young Professor. Our Professor was right, they do not resemble this Viennese Herr Professor Sigmund Freud. He is nearer to the grandfather and that religion, 'an atmosphere....'

They were North-of-England people. We children were the ninth generation to inherit a quaint English name. Six generations were weathered and shaped by the rock and flint of *New* England. Our father's father, the seventh, was lured with that covered wagon generation to the west. His young wife was not happy. They intended to get to California but they settled in Indiana. They began all over again, where the first Puritans of their name had started.

There were still a few Indians in the district. Our grandfather had his law books. Our father helped in the fields but he found plowing difficult. His idea of a straight line was more abstract; he had his father's Euclid.

They were hunting runaway slaves. Our young father missed the 'surge and thunder' of the New England odyssey. He looked to the heavens; mariners steer ships by stars.

He worked with lathe and saw, he was apprenticed to a carpenter. He learned his trade; his thin fingers had a 'feel' for pine, tulip-tree, and cedar. His sister Rosa appropriated the Virgil and translated for him. He did not know what he wanted when he picked out, with his far-sighted grey eyes, the ten stars of the Dipper or the eight of Orion's sword-belt. But he knew this satisfied him. He found Algol.

His brother Alvan was two years older. Alvan called to his brother, loitering as usual, in the darkness. There was a new call from Lincoln. Alvan said, 'I'm going.'

Charles went with him.

The younger of the two boys came back. He had no words with which to tell his mother of those last scenes, when she asked him. He had never laughed much. Now he tried to laugh it off, a raw imitation of Alvan's contagious laughter.

Alvan was dead. He hadn't been shot through with a bullet. They were rotting . . . they were . . . it was typhoid. 'It was quick,' he told his mother. He tried to remember something from Lincoln's last speech, he could only remember 'a great battlefield of this war,' but it wasn't a battlefield of war, not of this war . . . he knew that his mother felt now that a million free emancipated darkies weren't worth Alvan. Or didn't she? It was better not to know what she was thinking. He knew his mother was trying to love him, he had made that effort to come back to tell her . . . what he never told her.

He hadn't got a single reb, he told his father. Celia wished he wouldn't laugh in that way, so unlike Alvan, she felt he would choke. The elder Charles felt something of it. He asked Celia to fetch the Bible. 'Sweeter than honey in the honeycomb,' he read, opening it anywhere. Celia wished the boy wouldn't stare so. How could he tell his mother of the makeshift camp-hospital . . . at the end, there wasn't anyone left. . . . He crawled through some trees. He remembered juniper, birch, balm, and hickory. He muttered these clean words under his breath like a prayer. Alvan was dead. He must get back home somehow, to tell them. . . . 'The rebs left just as we got there, the camp –' His father went on reading, 'Yea, than much fine gold.'

He was shaken with the after-effects of the malaria and could scarcely stand up. Every time his eyes met Celia's he saw Alvan. He knew Celia saw Alvan too. Why had he come back? Why did we ever come west, thought Celia. That knocking? It was some friendly neighbor, they were all too friendly. She almost dropped the pan of corncake; it was the thud-thud of a hoe or maybe that colt loose again from the meadow. It might even be the kitchen clock; its tick was so loud she never noticed the clock back home. Slow now, if you stopped to listen. Time was so slow now. She could scream when she saw, through the open window, Charles sprawled out on the porch steps. He couldn't yet drag his shambling length after the plow.

He had taken his grandfather's old bubble-watch and laid it on the floorboards. What was he doing, chalking a clock-face round the bubble-watch? A stick was dangling from a string. It was fastened to the hook in the ceiling where Mercy had had her swing. Rosa was off, upstate to learn to be a teacher. Mercy was dead. There was no one here to help her. What was he doing marking along the shadow where the sun fell, with that chalk? Had he gone mad?

How old was Charles now? He was seventeen when he went with Alvan and lied about it, so they took him. Mercy and he had paired off together. Alvan and Rosa. She remembered how she had had to reprove Mercy for sing-songing, when it came her turn for reading.

The Bible was for decorum.

16

MARCH 22, WEDNESDAY, 6:30 P.M.

I GAVE THE PROFESSOR Bryher's books. He seemed rather professional and aloof after using half my session yesterday in gossip. I tell him last night's dream: hotel, stranger, dark (or in-the-dark) young man in the hall, he passes the open door and sees me. I wear a rose-colored picture-gown or ball-gown. I am pleased that he sees me and pose or sway as if forward to a dance. In a moment, he has caught me, I am lost (found?), we sway together like butterflies. He says, 'You *do* know how to dance.'

Now we go out together but I am in evening-dress, that is, I wear clothes like his. (I had been looking at some new pictures of Marlene Dietrich, in one of the café picture-papers.) I am not quite comfortable, not quite myself, my trouser-band does not fit very well; I realize that I have on, underneath the trousers, my ordinary underclothes, or rather I was wearing the long party-slip that apparently belonged to the ball-gown. The dream ends on a note of frustration and bewilderment.

This dream seems to have some association with Ezra; though he danced so badly, I did go to school-girl dances with him. The Professor knew the name, Ezra Pound. He said he had seen an article, but could not pretend to follow it. I told the Professor how Ezra had been more or less 'forbidden the house,' and the conflict at that time with my parents.

8:20 P.M.
I feel old. When I told the Professor of a much younger admirer of mine who had flattered and mildly 'courted' me, the Professor said, 'Was that *only* two years ago,' as if at my age (forty-six) I should be well over that sort of trifling. But I remembered the novel *Wagadoo* that Dr. Sachs brought us to read. As I remember, the woman in the book began her analysis at forty-seven . . . and she was at that age deeply involved in various love experiences or experiments. But that was French. Vienna, too, develops differently. The Professor seemed to be surprised when I told him that my first serious love-conflict or encounter was with Ezra when I was nineteen; he said then, 'As late as nineteen?' Perhaps, this is some technical mannerism or *façon de parler*.

Ezra and I took long walks; I remember the hepaticas, the spring is late in America, at least compared with England. I was triumphant if I found my first cluster of blue flowers or a frail stalk of wood anemone or bloodroot, the last day or one of the last days of March. To find flowers in March was a great triumph for us there.

I had not time to speak of my dream of the two Japanese-like dwarfs. Their surname is Anemone. (Japanese anemones . . . Bryher brought them to me several times a week at St. Faith's Nursing Home before my child was born; they are associated particularly with that time.) I discuss the dwarfs with my mother and we are both annoyed that they should have that flower-name.

17

MARCH 23, 8:45 P.M.

I STARTED TO HOLD FORTH on Frazer and *The Golden Bough*. The Professor waved me to the couch, 'More confession?' I said, no, I wanted to go over some of the old ground again. 'I will go back to Van Eck, do you remember Van Eck?' He said, 'Of course.' I told him that I felt reticent and shy coming back to all this. I told him of the crystal arriving in the State Express Cigarette box and a letter that I received, sent by Van Eck from Alexandria. I was then at Mullion Cove, Cornwall, with Bryher. The box had come to the new furnished flat we had found at Buckingham Mansions, Kensington, the preceding summer. It was the summer before this, July 1919, that we had gone first to the Scilly Isles together. The crystal seemed to carry out my vision or state of transcendental imagination when I had felt myself surrounded, as it were, with the two halves of the bell-jar.

I told the Professor how after some years I had met the cousin of Van Eck, or rather her sister, to whom he had written a letter, enclosed in this Mullion Cove note to me. I presented the letter, or sent it rather with a small book of my poems, but

Miss Van Eck never answered. Then, I met her sister in the Hotel Washington, Curzon Street, where I stayed when I went over to London.

I was now under the impression that Van Eck had been a total illusion or figment of my imagination, but when I mentioned him, and his helping Bryher on the boat with her Greek, to the younger Miss Van Eck, she said, 'Yes, he always was very good at languages.' So, there actually was a Van Eck and this lady and the elder, whom I had not met, were in fact his cousins.

Now there is a Van Eck. In my Hotel Washington bedroom, I pick up the telephone book. It did not occur to me before this that he might be back in England. But there was the odd distinguished and unusual name. I asked for the number and in no time at all a voice answered. It was a Belsize Park telephone number. The strange voice said, rather curtly I felt, 'Do you want Mr. or *Mrs.* Van Eck?'

This was a great shock to me. I was due to leave for Paris the next day. I managed somehow to get away. I met Bryher there. She said the shock was really a secondary one; that is, she felt I had superimposed it on the first shock of the parting from Aldington before we went to Greece.

But the Van Eck mystery still continues to obsess me. Again in London, from my Sloane Street flat, I consult a telephone book; there is Van Eck again, with another number.

It appears to be a City number, I judge an office. I will be ready now for any shock, but a pleasant young voice answers; he will give my number to Mr. Van Eck when he gets back to the office. Van Eck rings me. He comes to see me. I have other people in, Kenneth and Bryher, a strange girl who was sent to me from New York, a writer of sorts, pretty, in summer frock. This must be Van Eck, but I doubt if I would have known him had we met on the street.

18

THEN I GO ON with the Van Eck saga. I receive a card, spring 1931, when I am staying near Miss Chadwick in a big room in Tavistock Square. We get the connection with the maternal uncle, the gifted younger musician brother of my mother's Frederick... Van Eck.

This card is a notification or invitation to attend the church service at which Mr. Van Eck is to be ordained – I believe that is the word. It seemed an odd *volte-face*.

However, there was the name, the card, the statement of his new choice of career, the words, 'Pray for me.'

When I go back to my flat again in Sloane Street, I write again. Mr. Van Eck comes to call, a friend is with me, the Dorothy of the earlier Joan and Dorothy dream.

Now Mr. Van Eck disappears but I am at least informed of his intention. He is going for a time into 'retreat' in a High Church or Anglo-Catholic St. Francis of Assisi foundation in Dorset.

The Professor said these details only confirmed him in his first impression, or opinion, that the Van Eck episode or fixation was to be referred back to my mother. The maternal uncle, church, art.

The Professor asked me if I had ever wanted to go on the stage. He said he felt I narrated these incidents so dramatically, as if I had 'acted them out' or 'prepared' before coming to him. I told the Professor how I loved 'dressing up,' but most children do. There were some old stage properties in our first home, left to my mother by a retired prima donna who had taught singing at the old school where my grandfather was. The Professor said he felt some sort of 'resistance.'

I felt exhausted and restless. I made myself a hot lemon drink in my bedroom and took cibalgine . . . a good night's rest. It was blighting cold but I got out later in the morning in the sun.

19

AGAIN, THE PROFESSOR ASKED ME if I 'prepared' for my sessions with him. I said I had been writing letters up to the last. I had had a dream of the sea, fear . . . and this connected with my youngest brother, who had been 'the baby.'

Yes, we had had school entertainments if that was 'acting.' There was a Kate Greenaway pageant or sequence and I had a poem to recite, 'My Garden is Under the Window.' There was (the next year) *Mother Goose* but I was disappointed in my Miss Muffet spider rôle. The younger brother wore the Boy Blue costume that I afterwards appropriated. The older one was rather magnificent as King Cole.

I mentioned the circus 'lady' who was 'dressed up' in tights, taming the lions.

At school, when I was fifteen, one of the girls, half-French, whose name Moffat rather, now, recalls that other Miss Muffet disappointment. But with Renée I was featured as the hero in most of the plays or charades she arranged for us. Renée had seen Sarah Bernhardt in *L'Aiglon* and would act out whole scenes. The Professor suggested that I visit Schönbrun, and see for myself the apartments of the Duc de Reichstadt.

The Professor repeated that he wanted the work to be spontaneous. He does not encourage me to take notes, in fact, would rather I did not.

I went on with Renée. Her name was Renée Athené, she

had been born in Athens where her father was in one of the services. It was at her house that I had my first (and last) experience with table-tapping. I must say very little came of it. But this period, early adolescence, was a return to happy childhood. My mother had Halloween games, fortune telling 'for fun,' and various games such as telling the future from a small candle-end stuck in a nutshell that was set afloat on a tub of water. These games were only played at Halloween. Renée pretended to see a ghost – perhaps she did see one – that Halloween when I first went to Miss Gordon's school. Her name of course fascinated me; very soon after this, I saw my first real Greek play, done by students at the university. Still later, my friend Frances Josepha, with whom I first came to Europe, showed me beautiful photographs of herself in Greek costume; she had been a boy or youth in some play.

Now I remember Anny Ahlers and how I heard her sing, with Dorothy (of the dream) in London. She stepped from a window. I read this in my usual café picture-paper. It was du Barry she was playing. She might, too, have been in *L'Aiglon*.

The only actual experience I had with 'ghosts' was in Cornwall, the last war-year. But these presences, these 'knockers' were famous, everybody heard them.

I recall, for some reason, the Siena wolf. Remus was the legendary founder of Siena. Perhaps, I am thinking of the lost companion, the sister that I never had, a twin sister best of all.

We discussed Greek names, commonly used; Helen, my mother, Ida our nurse, now this Renée Athené.

Renée's mother taught the smaller children French at Miss Gordon's. Frances' mother was supervisor of kindergartens in Philadelphia. My own mother taught music and drawing at the old Seminary in Bethlehem.

The Greek came most vividly to me when I was seven; it was a Miss Helen who read us *Tanglewood Tales*, Friday afternoon at school. Those stories are my foundation or background, Pandora, Midas, the Gorgon-head — that particular story of Perseus and the guardian, Athené.

The miracle of the fairy-tale is incontrovertible; Sigmund Freud would apply, rationalize it.

WEDNESDAY, JUNE 12, 1933

I leave Vienna, Saturday of this week.

I discontinued the notes, at the Professor's suggestion.

We repeated and worked through more of the detail of the first Greek trip and my dream of hallucination of the dolphins and the 'double' Van Eck.

We went over the Egyptian trip too, the opening of the tomb, Luxor and Philae.

I dream of two books; I have written them. 'I have this book coming out,' I say; then, 'I have a second book to follow.'

The Professor says that Athené is the veiled Isis, or Neith the warrior-goddess. He found and placed the small statue of Athené in my hands. There is another Athené, or winged Niké, on the vase that we looked at, when I was describing my Writing on the Wall.

I remembered again the lion-headed Sekmet and spoke of a cat-carving we found on the Acropolis.

JUNE 15

Continued rumors are perhaps responsible for last night's dream, a nightmare. An enormous black buffalo, bison, or bull is pursuing a cart or carriage in which we are all crowded.

Had the car plunged over a cliff? Were we in it?

Some of us, a group of six or eight, now seated on a mountain slope, ask, *are we dead?*

APPENDIX

FREUD'S LETTERS TO H.D.

READING THE LETTERS from Freud to H.D., one early winter's day in Switzerland, where she then lived, it was clear to me that they properly belonged in an appendix to her homage to 'the Professor.' Not as affidavit, but as an extension of that companionable warmth which Freud extended toward the creative spirit and its search for identity and direction.

So I asked H.D. for the privilege of printing the letters here, and then, later, secured permission from Freud's heirs for those which they selected from the number he had written her. Of these nine letters which they chose, the ones dated July 20, 1933; December 28, 1935; May 1936; September 20, 1936; and February 26, 1937, were written in German and are printed in a translation by Annemarie Holborn. The others are in Freud's own English. All of these letters in the appendix are included 'By Permission of Sigmund Freud Copyrights Ltd.'

N.H.P.

Dec. 18th, 1932
Wien IX., *Berggasse 19*

Dear Mrs. Aldington

I am not sure of your knowing German so I beg to accept my bad English. It may be especially trying to a poet.

You will understand that I did not ask for your books in order to criticize or to appreciate your work, which I have been informed is highly

·189·

praised by your readers. I am a bad judge on poetry especially in a foreign language. I wanted to get a glimpse of your personality as an introduction to making your personal acquaintance. Your books will be waiting with me for your arrival. (An American friend of mine brought me today 'Palimpsest.')

My relations to my patients (or pupils) are now especially complicated. I hope to arrange them in a few weeks and I will make an effort not to let you stay in waiting very long.

With kind regards
yours sincerely
Freud

26 January 1933
Wein IX., *Berggasse 19*

Dear Madam

I did not answer the charming letter you wrote to me late in December. At that time I hoped to be able to call you here very soon. But things have turned out differently. I did not succeed in finding time for you and kept postponing a decision. Now your second letter has reached me, together with the book on H. Ellis, which shall wait here for your arrival. I understand that a certain delay was quite agreeable to you. But I do not want to extend it too long, and I have made up my mind to make the necessary arrangements, even if it means using force. On the other hand, I cannot expect you to travel or change your place of residence in this present biting cold and at a time when an epidemic of grippe is spreading. I have heard that you are of delicate health. Would you prefer to come at the beginning of spring, in April/May? It is hard to control these hygienic factors and easy to make miscalculations.

Sachs wrote about you and your friends from Boston. I have not heard from H. Ellis – I owned already the book in honor of his seventieth birth-

day and have taken note of who is meant by the lofty person of the revelation.

> *With kindest regards to you and your friends,*
> *Yours,*
> *Freud*

P.S. Glad you understand German.

> *20 July 1933*
> *Wien IX., Berggasse 19*

Dear H.D.

Thank you for your long letter which was written under such sad circumstances. I have already had a letter from Bryher from London. Probably the future depends on how Lady E. will feel. I talked to Yo and Tattoun: 'You careless pack, you do not realize that Sir John is dead and that you may never have Perdita as your foster-mother nor see Villa Kenwin.' Since you have to part with them and this parting is very hard on you, you wish at least to see them in good hands. There has been much commotion in the dog-state. Wulf had to be shipped off to Kagran, because both ladies were in heat, and the fierce antagonism between Yofi and Lün, which is rooted in the nature of women, resulted in good, gentle Lün's being bitten by Yofi. Thus Lün, too, is at present in Kagran and her future is uncertain.

About the human occupants of the house I can only report that they have been ill much of the time and only now begin to enjoy the summer.

I confidently expected to hear from you that you are writing, but such matter should never be forced. I trust I shall hear so later on.

The Spanish adventure about which you report is terrible and mysterious. . . .

> *With kindest regards,*
> *Yours,*
> *Freud*

March 5th 1934
Wien IX., *Berggasse 19*

Dear H.D.!

    Is it really a whole year since you first called on me? Yes, and the second half of this term I spent in suffering owing to the bad effects of another slight operation which was intended to relieve my habitual ailings. But after all it was not a tragic affair, only the inevitable expression of old age and the degeneration of tissues dependent on it. So I do not complain. I know I am overdue and whatever I still have is an unexpected gift.

    Nor is it too painful a thought to leave this scene and set of phenomena for good. There is not much left to be regretted, times are cruel and the future appears to be disastrous. For a while we were afraid we will not be able to stay in this town and country – it is unpleasant to go into exile at the age of seventy-eight – but now we think we have escaped at least this danger.

    We passed through a week of civil war. Not much personal suffering, just one day without electric light, but the 'stimmung' was awful and the feeling as of an earthquake. No doubt, the rebels belonged to the best portion of the population, but their success would have been very short-lived and brought about military invasion of the country. Besides they were Bolshevists and I expect no salvation from Communism. So we could not give our sympathy to either side of the combatants.

    I am sorry to hear you do not yet work but according to your own account the forces are seething. From Perdita's trip, I am getting postcards. The last came from Trinidad. Happy girl!

    Give my love to Bryher and don't forget me.

Yours affectionately
Freud

28 December 1935
Wien IX., Berggasse 19

Dear H.D. and Perdita:

I think I shall prefer to continue in German. We here, too, have more fog and darkness than is usual around Christmas time. But in front of my window in the inner room stands a proud, sweet-smelling plant. Only twice have I seen it in bloom in a garden, at the Lago di Garda and in the Val Lugano. It reminds me of those bygone days when I was still able to move around and visit the sunshine and beauty of southern nature myself. It is a datura, a noble relative of the tobacco plant, whose leaves used to do so much for me in former times but now can do so little.

It is hardly advisable to give an octogenarian something beautiful. There is too much sadness mixed in with the enjoyment. But one thing is certain: I have not deserved this gift from you and Perdita, since I did not even answer your friendly letters regularly.

I sincerely return your kind wishes for a good year 1936. You, and especially Perdita, still have so much ahead of you. I hope there will be much that is good and liberating. Also Bryher must allow me to thank her at least in this connection.

In warm friendship,
yours,
Freud

May 1936

MY SINCERE THANKS FOR YOUR KIND
REMEMBRANCE ON THE OBSERVANCE
OF MY EIGHTIETH BIRTHDAY

Your Freud

Will you forgive me this barbaric reaction to such loving expressions [of friendship]? I am sure Yofi is very proud of being mentioned by you. Believe it or not, early on the sixth she came into my bedroom to show me her affection in her own fashion, something she has never done before or after. How does a little animal know when a birthday comes around?

24 May 1936
XIX *Strasserg 47*
Wien IX., *Berggasse 19*

Dear H.D.

All your white cattle safely arrived lived and adorned the room up to yesterday.

I had imagined I had become insensitive to praise and blame. Reading your kind lines and getting aware of how I enjoyed them I first thought I had been mistaken about my firmness. Yet on second thoughts I concluded I was not. What you gave me, was not praise, was affection and I need not be ashamed of my satisfaction.

Life at my age is not easy, but spring is beautiful and so is love.

Yours affectionately
Freud

20 September 1936
Wien IX., *Berggasse 19*

Belated, though sincere, congratulations on the occasion of your fiftieth birthday from an eighty-year-old friend.

Fr.

26 February 1937
Wien IX., *Berggasse 19*

Dear H.D.

I have just finished your Ion. *Deeply moved by the play (which I had not known before) and no less by your comments, especially those referring to the end, where you extol the victory of reason over passions, I send you the expression of my admiration and kindest regards,*

Yours,
Freud